LESSONS LEARNED
Along the Way
From INDIANA to INDONESIA

WAYNE W. ALLEN

Xulon
PRESS

To my children and grandchildren

ENDORSEMENT

Dr. Wayne Allen's book reads like pages out of the book of Acts in the Bible. God still speaks, calls, equips, and commissions people to His harvest fields just as He did in the book of Acts. You will be challenged to true discipleship and to take up your cross to follow Jesus as you read of Dr. Allen's conversion experience and the stories of his experiences on the mission field in Asia. This book challenged me to return to the discipline of prayer as a priority and reminded me that I am here to do God's will, not mine. If you are satisfied with the status quo, do not read this book! But if you wish to become a radical disciple of Christ, read this book to fuel your desire to be set ablaze for Christ.

C. Ruth Taylor
Author, Former Missionary with Operation
Mobilization

CONTENTS

FOREWORD

O ne of the most important things I learned from
working among the Dayaks of West Kalimantan,
Indonesia, was the importance of telling stories. I was
trained in propositional and exegetical preaching in
Bible college. Good sermons always consisted of, I was
taught, a thesis statement and three supporting arguments. The thesis should grow directly out of the biblical text. The supporting arguments should grow out of
the exegesis of the text, and this required in-depth study
of the original language of the text. I learned to despise
sermons that consisted of many stories instead of solid
biblical exegesis.

Soon after I began preaching in West Kalimantan
I discovered that my exegetical sermons did not have
the same powerful impact as the sermons of my colleagues. As I investigated the reasons for this, I noticed
that the sermons that had the greatest impact on Dayak
audiences were filled with stories. I recognized I had
to adjust my preaching style if I was to be an effective
witness of the gospel of Jesus Christ. The propositional
statements and the exegesis had to be combined with

stories that illustrated the truth of, and the application of, the propositions presented in the sermon.

As I improved my use of this new style of sermon, I recognized that people remembered my theses longer and with greater clarity when I linked them with a story. As I used the stories of my work in West Kalimantan to explain Christian truth in the United States, folks began to urge me to write a book sharing these stories because the stories taught important lessons. I did not want to write a book of stories, though. I wanted to teach people to be better disciples of Jesus Christ. I was not interested in writing a book just to tell my stories.

Then one day I met a Batak Christian in Medan who asked me two very difficult questions. First, why are American Christians able to send missionaries, but Batak Christians cannot? Second, how did you evangelize the Dayaks of West Kalimantan? As I contemplated these questions, I recognized that my stories illustrated the biblical truths that provide answers to these questions, and thus I came to write this book.

My thesis is that missionary service, by Christians of any ethnic group, is just basic discipleship. It is life lived by the principle of the cross as presented by Jesus in Matthew 16:24, Mark 8:34, and Luke 14:27. Christians often misunderstand the principle of the cross. They commonly think that it means one must be willing to die for Christ but overlook the requirement of being willing to live for Christ. In this book I explain what it means to live for Christ as a missionary, and how the Dayaks were evangelized, by using these stories.

In Part 1, The Basis of Discipleship, I demonstrate from my own experience that a missionary must know God has called him to that task. I tell the story of how

God called me to missions and specifically to West Kalimantan and confirmed it with three signs. The stories demonstrate the proposition that a missionary is simply a disciple of Jesus who has taken up his cross and followed Him. I explain that a missionary must understand why God sent him to a certain place. I demonstrate this with two stories about my motorcycle travels in West Kalimantan and a story of a difficult ministry experience. Again, these stories demonstrate the proposition.

In Part 2, The Power of Discipleship, I present three types of prayer that are essential to successful missionary service. These types of prayer are illustrated by three stories from my personal missionary experience.

In Part 3, The Methods of Discipleship, I demonstrate how we did missions in West Kalimantan with the story of my ministry trip into the Sekayam River valley. The story demonstrates that our missionary method was based on two principles: preach the gospel and bless the community.

Throughout this work the propositional statements and the exegesis of the principle of the cross are combined with personal life stories. The stories illustrate the truth of, and the application of, the principle of the cross. It is my conviction that the principle of the cross explains why American Christians are able to send missionaries. The stories also demonstrate how the team with which I worked was able to evangelize Dayaks in West Kalimantan.

My hope and prayer is that these stories will motivate many Christians to answer the call of Christ to take up their cross, and to follow Jesus' example of making disciples who make disciples.

INTRODUCTION

A colleague serving the Body of Christ in Medan arranged for me to speak to a number of churches in the city over a period of several days. While returning from ministry one morning, he asked me to wait while he took care of some business with a local publisher. While waiting, I had the privilege of meeting the owner of the publishing company. The owner was surprised that I was able to speak Indonesian and asked where I learned the language. Learning of my thirteen years in the interior of West Kalimantan, he wanted to know about my life and work there.

He asked many questions. With which ethnic group were you working? How did you plant a church without a church building, formal liturgy, or ordained clergy? How did you make disciples without a catechism? Who did the baptisms and served Holy Communion? How did you teach them about Jesus, salvation, the Trinity, and the Holy Spirit? Who taught the Sunday school?

I tried to give simple answers, but he would not accept them. He wanted details. He was a skilled interviewer, and he knew the Scriptures. His questions required thoughtful, precise answers.

As we talked, his questions turned to the personal aspects of ministry. How long did you work there? Where did you live? What was your house like? What did you, an American, eat? How did you learn to live in the jungle without electricity? Where did your children go to school? How did your parents deal with you taking their grandchildren so far away from them?

But there was one question to which he often returned, that he asked several times: Why are you Americans able to send missionaries around the world but we Batak Christians cannot do so? It was a hard question to answer without sounding like an arrogant American Christian who thinks he has all the answers to the world's problems. I replied in general terms. I did not want to offend my host by a poorly considered comment. But when it came time to leave, he urged me to write the story of my work in West Kalimantan.

"Our people need to hear this story," he said. "We need to know how you evangelized the Dayaks."

I replied that it was something I had considered, but I did not think anyone was interested. I did not think there was a market for such a story.

"You write it," he said, "and I will publish it. Our people need to hear this. The generations to come need to know what it took to establish the Church of God in West Kalimantan. We also need to know why you Americans are able to send missionaries around the world but we Batak Christians cannot do so."

I began to think about how to tell the story of the evangelization of the Dayaks in West Kalimantan. I could not tell the whole story, of course. I could only tell what I had seen and done in the areas where I had served. There is a much larger story to be told, but I doubt any single person can tell that story. Those who worked in the various parts of the province must write their stories. Then, sometime in the future, one of God's servants will be anointed to compile the smaller accounts into one larger history of the growth of the Kingdom of God in West Kalimantan.

However, I began to consider how I would tell story. I realized there are certain basic principles of ministry that must be presented. A missionary is simply a disciple of Jesus Christ fulfilling the call of God on his life. Not all disciples are called to be missionaries, but all who put their faith in Jesus are called to discipleship.

I believe there are three aspects of discipleship that are essential to successful missionary service. First, the basis of discipleship is the call of God. No one stays on the mission field without a clear call and a deep commitment to God's work. Without it, people quit and go home.

Second, the power of discipleship is prayer. Prayer is essential to successful discipleship—especially to missionary service. While there are many ways to pray, the critical issue is that one prays! Without a strong prayer life, again, people quit and go home.

Third, methods of discipleship are varied and can best be presented by simply telling the stories of what was done. The methods we used were traditional ones. They were effective. These methods can best be presented by telling the stories of what we did and what happened when we did it.

This led me to consider how I would present these principles. Clearly, stories are the best way to present the methodology, but what about the basis and the power of discipleship? Some basic principles can be presented by propositional teaching. American theologians love propositional preaching and teaching. It is powerful and effective. However, my experience in Asia taught me that Asians are not as enamored of propositional preaching as Americans.

Dayaks and other ethnic groups whom I taught in India, Nepal, Bhutan, Bangladesh, and Myanmar preferred stories over propositional teaching. The stories brought the principles and propositions to life. It gave real and practical illustrations of difficult concepts. The Dayaks did not like the long lists of propositions that are so often presented in theology texts, but they were drawn to stories presenting the same truths.

This book is my attempt to answer the key questions that concerned my publisher friend in Medan. Why are Americans able to send missionaries around the world? First, I think they can do so because they understand and embrace the principle of the cross. This is foundational to all discipleship and Christian ministry. This understanding leads the believer to accept the call of God for ministry in a new culture. I demonstrate this from my personal experience in Part 1: The Basis of Discipleship.

Second, American disciples understand that nothing happens in Christian discipleship apart from prayer. Truly, prayer is the power of discipleship and missionary service. It enables the disciple to understand God's plans and purposes in a given event. It strengthens the will of the disciple in the face of culture shock, in the search for God's will, and in learning to trust Him in the darkest moments of life and service. I demonstrate this with personal experiences in Part 2: The Power of Discipleship.

Finally, the methods of discipleship are as varied as the languages of the world. Every culture expresses itself in a unique way in its own language. Every culture, and the language that expresses it, grows out of the environment and the interaction of its people with each other and with that environment. Presentations of the gospel must be done within that language and culture. This requires that a disciple who has been called by God to evangelize a new people group, a new culture, must begin by learning the language and the culture.

I could not explain the gospel in English in West Kalimantan. I had to learn to use the Indonesian language. I had to train Dayak disciples to explain the gospel in their languages—Bekua, Benana, Bernyadu, Belangin, and others.

Neither could I use gospel presentation methods I used in the United States. The Four Spiritual Laws were useful for a time in the United States, but they were not the best option in West Kalimantan. I learned through experience that stories held the attention of a typical Dayak villager far better than propositional laws and statements. I could tell the stories of Creation, the Fall, and Babel with far greater effect than I could explain the laws of the faith.

The methods I used are demonstrated in Part 3: The Methods of Discipleship as seen on the Sekayam River Trek. My emphasis was on preaching the gospel, leading folks to faith in Jesus, and training them to tell their story to their own people. I also wanted to assist their communities. My colleague on the trip was a registered nurse and his medical skill was a vivid example to the Dayaks that we were interested in their daily lives as well as in their spiritual destiny.

These are some of the lessons I learned along the way. As I was transformed by the power of the Holy Spirit and benefited from the patient coaching of my Dayak brothers in Christ, I learned to make disciples, bless their communities, and glorify God in West Kalimantan. I present these stories in the hope that they will inspire a new generation of disciples to deny their own personal goals, ambitions, plans, desires, and choices and replace them with an unrelenting, unchangeable commitment to the task to which God has called them.

Part 1

The Basis of Discipleship

Chapter 1

A PROPHET TO THE NATIONS

W hat motivates a person to leave their home, family, people, and culture? Some people cannot do it. Even in this modern, frenetic age when Americans change jobs every 4.4 years (on average) and job-hopping is considered normal many people cannot move far away from the area where they were raised.[1] Paul Emrath documented that in the United States, "roughly half of all single family home owners [have] lived in their homes for at least 10 years. There has been very little change in this percentage since 2003" (NAHB).[2] Like the Navaho, many simply cannot live at peace away from "their" land (Barboncito).[3] For most, it is not a spiritual matter as it was for the Navaho. It is more a sense of peace that comes from knowing the neighborhood, the community, the streets of the city; or the woods, fields, streams, and rivers of the farms. Even more, it is a sense of culture.

The culture provides a worldview, a belief system, a value system, a language, a social and political realm, and a way of life that a person understands. It makes the person feel comfortable, at ease, and at "home." It is a rare person who can set aside all these things, leave home, acquire a new culture, and thrive in that new culture.

The culture is powerful, and many cannot break free of it. This is why immigration is a vital concern in much of the world today. Immigrants to the nineteenth-century United States left behind the old ways, the old culture, and the old language. They adopted the language and culture of their new country. With the new worldview, belief system, and value system, they built a new nation based on freedom, personal initiative, and basic Christian morality. Now, in the twenty-first century, immigrants take their cultures with them. They refuse to adopt the new culture, preferring to retain their own worldview, beliefs, values, and language.

So, what motivates a person to leave home with the specific intent of acquiring a new language and culture? Simply stated, it is the call of God to His service. This is the basis of discipleship, accepting the call of God and embracing His goals, aims, plans, desires and choices for one's life. This is clearly demonstrated in my story.

I was raised in a Christian family. My mother accepted Jesus as her personal Savior in an evangelistic campaign in central Tennessee when she was sixteen years of age. The campaign was held in a church near her home, featuring the preaching of Rev. Harold Walker. My father came to Jesus as an adult, when I was already six years of age. After my father's conversion, our family changed. We began attending Harvester

Missionary Church in Fort Wayne, Indiana whenever the doors were open.

As a child I attended all the church services. On Sunday morning I attended Sunday school. There was a class for each age group, so my parents were in the adult class while I was in the children's class. After Sunday school, while my parents attended the worship service, I attended "Junior Church," a worship service designed especially for children ages five to twelve. On Sunday evenings I attended the "training hour" for children and youth. There was a class for ages five to twelve and a youth program for ages thirteen to eighteen. After the training hour, I joined my parents for the evangelistic service. The pastor would present a basic gospel message and always closed the service with an altar call, challenging believers present to greater holiness and service to God, and calling unbelievers to an initial profession of faith in Jesus.

Every autumn and every spring, the church would conduct two-week evangelistic programs. Evangelists would be invited to visit the church to conduct these campaigns. Every night for two weeks, except for Saturday night when folks needed to prepare for Sunday, the evangelist would preach powerful messages about the importance of receiving Jesus as one's personal savior. They would tell exciting stories about dramatic conversions and frightening stories of people refusing to repent, even on their deathbeds as visions of hell filled their minds during their last moments of life. In the days before television became common in the United States, these events were a welcomed change from the ordinary daily routine, so the meetings were always well attended. There was little else to do, so the whole community would come out to hear the preaching. My parents were committed to Christ, so we attended every service. Every one!

Every summer, soon after school was dismissed for the summer vacation, our church would conduct a two-week Vacation Bible School (VBS). Monday through Friday from 9:00 in the morning until noon, the community children would come to the church for singing, games, crafts, snacks, and, of course, Bible stories. A special speaker would be invited. The speaker was always a well-known children's minister. The speaker, man or woman, could tell stories that would hold the attention of the children. In the early years I was enthralled by the stories of people who had worked in Africa and Asia. They would often share stories of sick children who were healed by the work of American doctors and nurses or of children who were taught to read and write by Americans who served as missionaries around the world.

My father insisted I attend every service, program, and activity at the church. Whenever the doors were open, I had to be there. Over the years I learned all the Bible stories. I knew the story of creation, and how Cain murdered Abel. I knew the story of Noah and the ark. I even knew the names of his sons, and the places on the earth where their descendants lived up until the times of Abraham. I learned the stories of Abraham, Isaac, and Jacob. By the time I was twelve years of age, I could tell the story of David and Goliath from memory as the teacher told it to my Sunday school class. I knew about David and Jonathan and how Saul tried to kill David. I even knew how David spared Saul's life on two occasions. I knew all about the life and teaching of

Jesus, from his birth to his resurrection and ascension to heaven. I could recite the cities St. Paul visited on each of his missionary journeys and tell you what happened in each city. I could even recite the seven churches of Revelation and tell you what was wrong with each one. I knew all the stories—even Job's.

I had memorized all the important Bible verses, too. I knew Genesis 1:1 and 12:1. I knew the Ten Commandments. I knew the Hebrew confession that "The Lord is one" (Dt 6:4). I knew the Psalms, too—1, 23, 67, 100, 133, and more. I had memorized the Beatitudes (Mt 5:1–12), the Lord's Prayer, and John 3:16–17. I knew the Roman Road of Salvation—Romans 1:18, 3:23; 6:23; 10:9–10. As a teen I added Romans 12:1–2. I memorized the verses about taking up my cross, about Jesus taking my heavy burdens, about casting all my cares upon Jesus, and Jesus knocking on the door of my heart. I knew all the important verses—even 1 John 1:9.

I even knew all the stories the evangelists told. I had heard the same stories told by many different evangelists, so I knew them by heart. I could tell the stories at school on the playground. I could tell the stories about missionaries working in South America and even name the tribes they served when my school teachers asked about it. I was so bored hearing the same stories over and over that I finally told my parents, "I am not going to church anymore. I know all the stories and verses. I know all the stories the preachers tell. I don't need to hear them again, so I am not going to church anymore."

My mother was shocked and very upset, but my father handled the situation with his usual direct approach. He quietly picked me up off the floor by my shirt collar. With my feet dangling in the air, and his finger in my face, Dad said firmly, "You are going to church." He then put me on a chair and walked away. So, I went to church.

For the next five years I went to church only because my father was bigger and stronger than me. I had no desire to follow Jesus. I had no interest in the Bible. I wanted one thing more than anything else, and I was willing to do anything necessary to get it. I wanted money!

My family was poor. Dad worked hard, but the jobs he was able to get did not pay well. We had a house, food, and clothes, but that was it. There was no money for toys or games or ice cream. We had enough but no more. I wanted more. My friends had new bicycles, baseball gloves, basketballs, and many other things that I wanted. I could not have them because we did not have the money to buy them. I soon realized that if I wanted those things I would have to get them myself. So, I learned to steal.

I started with small things that I could fit in a pocket. A piece of candy was easy. I soon had pens and pencils for school in abundance. Rulers and triangles were needed for school, and soon I had plenty. I started to sell them to my classmates. I would steal them and sell them for half price. My classmates were happy. I was happy. I had money.

Soon I started to steal bigger things, like shirts and trousers. Again, I would steal what I could and keep what I wanted. What I did not want, I would sell to my friends for half price. My abundance of toys, clothes, and school supplies created another problem.

My mother soon asked where I got the new pens and pencils. These I explained away by saying, "I found them." But one does not find a new shirt at the park or on the street. I had to find better explanations—bigger lies. I became as good a liar as I was a thief.

So even though I went to church whenever the doors were open, I refused to accept Jesus as my personal savior. I was determined to have the money I needed to buy the things I wanted. I became known both at church and at school as a liar and a thief.

I did not care about my bad reputation. I only cared about the money and doing well at school. My grades were good. I was one of the smartest kids in my school. I determined that I would become an attorney because I believed they always had lots of money. As an attorney, I believed, I would be able to buy a big house, a fancy car, and have many girlfriends. I knew what I wanted out of life, and I knew how to get it. I did not need God, and I had no interest in the Bible or church. I still went to church, though, because Dad was still bigger and stronger than me.

Conversion

My life changed dramatically in November 1968. The autumn evangelistic crusade was going on at Harvester Church, and Rev. Harold Walker was preaching. This was the same man who preached the night my mother was saved when she was only sixteen years old. I had heard him before and knew him to be a colorful and energetic preacher, but on this Sunday night, the last night of the crusade, I was only present because my father made me go.

I sat in the back of the church, near the door. I planned to wait until my father was listening to the preacher, and then I would sneak out the back. I watched carefully, but every time I thought I could leave, my father would turn and look at me from his seat in the front of the church. I realized that if I left, Dad would know. So I was forced to remain in the service. I did not listen to anything that was said, and I have no idea what Rev. Walker preached that night. I just know that God spoke to me during the altar call.

As I stood in the back of the church, with the congregation singing one of the traditional altar-call hymns, I heard someone call my name. I looked around to see who it was but saw no one. The benches behind me were empty. Again, I heard someone call my name, but I saw no one. When the voice called a third time, I knew God was talking to me.

God said, "This is your last chance to repent and give your life to me. You are to become a missionary. You are to attend Fort Wayne Bible College. You are to marry Carolyn Paxson. If you do not repent and accept my will for your life tonight, I will never call you again. This is your last opportunity to receive salvation."

I argued with Him. I told him I was the bad kid—a liar and a thief. I was unfit to be a missionary. He should get one of the good kids in the group. They would be happy to be a missionary. I told Him I did not want to do this, that I was unfit for His service, and that he should call someone else. I told Him I was too bad to be a missionary, no Bible college would admit me with my reputation, and Carolyn Paxson would not even talk to me because she was a good girl and she knew my reputation as a liar and a thief.

God again spoke to me. "Wayne," he said, "Either you repent tonight and give your life to Me for missionary service or you will never be saved. You will die in your sins." At that point I yielded to Him. I went forward to the altar to confess my sins, to tell the church that I was converted, and to begin a new life of holiness and devotion to God.

I began my new life of pursuing holiness the very next morning. I had been attending church for twelve years, so I knew that a Christian should have personal devotions every morning. Rising thirty minutes earlier than usual, I sat at my desk to begin my personal devotions. Just as I had been taught in Sunday school, I started with prayer.

I asked God to guide me and talk to me as I read the Bible. I wanted to study something I had never read or studied before, so I opened my Bible to Jeremiah and began to read. God answered my prayer as these words seemed to have been written just for me. They spoke to me personally, as if God was once again speaking to me with an audible voice. He gave me Jeremiah 1:5 as my life verse.

> Before I formed you in the womb I knew you:
> Before you were born I sanctified you:
> I ordained you a prophet to the nations.

This confirmed what He told me the previous night. I was to be a missionary, a prophet to the nations. Like St. Paul, "I was not disobedient to the heavenly vision" (Acts 26:19).

After more than forty years of missionary service, I have never heard of another servant of Christ who had a similar experience of debating with God. It seems to be an experience unique to me alone. However, every missionary with whom I have discussed this has shared that he or she had the same sense of God's calling to ministry. Like me, every one of them knew, with absolute certainty, that God had called them to discipleship as a missionary. The manner of the calling is secondary to the fact of the calling. Without that certainty of God's call, the disciple fails to endure in missionary service.

College

The way forward was not easy, nor was it straight. I still had hopes of pursuing a career as an attorney. When I graduated from high school, instead of enrolling in Fort Wayne Bible College as I knew God had instructed me to do, I enrolled in Indiana University at its Fort Wayne campus. In my heart I was hoping that God would forget about calling me to missions. I tried to persuade God to allow me to be a Christian attorney, with hopes of pursuing a political career. I thought that as a Christian attorney I could be a positive influence in the legal and political realms. In my philosophy class, though, I learned that this was a futile idea.

My Introduction to Philosophy course was designed to demonstrate that humanity did not need God. The instructor reviewed the great philosophers of the ages, from Socrates to Kierkegaard. He required that the students read the best of these philosophers' writings and then discuss them in class. I made it my mission to demonstrate that the Christian worldview and philosophy of life was superior to all offered by these non-Christian perspectives. I consistently presented the view that these men were foolish, not wise, because they were trying to achieve what God had already done—explain good and evil and motivate humanity to reject evil and embrace good.

My instructor was not impressed by my arguments. I had learned enough of the Christian faith that I could answer all of his arguments against it. I could also point out the fallacies of his hero, Joseph Fletcher, and his "situational ethics." He argued that situational ethics, without any moral absolutes, would lead to a better, more tolerant society. I argued that it would lead to chaos, mass murder, infanticide, euthanasia, and the breakdown of society. The issue came to a climax when he refused to grade my essay submitted as the second test for the course.

The test question was simple. "Write and explain your moral code." So I wrote the Ten Commandments, and explained them from a basic literal-grammatical hermeneutical perspective. It was the work of a college freshman, but I still think I did a good job explaining the basics of right and wrong, good and evil, based on these commandments. The instructor was not impressed.

He refused to grade my work, claiming that I was talking religion, not philosophy. I renewed my argument that philosophy was merely religion developed without God. For two hours I sat in his office and argued that my paper should be accepted and graded fairly. His instruction was to write my moral code. I had done so, with excellence I believed, and I was entitled to a perfect score on my test. He maintained I was talking religion, not philosophy, and deserved a failing grade on the test. We finally agreed that my test would not be graded. My final grade for the course would be based on two exams, the first exam, which was already in the grade book, and the third, or final, exam. It was the best I could get from him.

The course and the interaction with the professor taught me two significant things that impacted my future life and ministry. First, I no longer wanted to pursue a legal or political career. The complete lack of moral absolutes, of any clear definition of right or wrong, made it impossible to adjudicate anything. Right or wrong was dependent on the opinion of the ruling power—the judge, the mass media, and/or the political power controlling the government. Truth no longer mattered. Only power and the ability to justify what one wanted to do truly mattered. I knew if I worked in that system, I would succumb to the temptations of money and power and would end up in jail for breaking the law.

Second, I learned to despise political, philosophical, and theological debate. Such debates are pointless because both sides are absolutely convinced their view is correct. Nothing the other side presents will convince one of the error of his point of view. All it will do is convince one side that they did not make a strong argument. I determined to study the Scriptures until I fully understood them. Then I would preach those things that I knew to be true. The things I did not know for certain, I would acknowledge and continue to study; but I would not present them as settled truth.

These two things convinced me I was in the wrong school. The following academic year I transferred to Fort Wayne Bible College. This fulfilled the first of the signs God gave me at my conversion. The next sign was my marriage to Carolyn Paxson.

Carolyn

Carolyn began attending Harvester Church when she was two weeks old. Her mother was a charter member of the church, was married in the church, and attended Harvester all her life. Carolyn was dedicated to Christ in the church. Carolyn attended church faithfully because her parents were committed to Christ and to Harvester church.

Carolyn attended all the children's programs, Sunday school, Vacation Bible School, and youth programs. Like me, whenever the church doors were open, she was present. Her parents raised her to love Jesus and to do what was right. She was a good girl. She accepted Jesus as her Savior in her early years, and by her twelfth birthday, she knew that God had called her to be a missionary.

In those days the boys and girls had separate Sunday school classes on Sunday morning but were in one group for the Sunday evening children and youth training hours. We knew each other from attending various children and youth activities, but it was not until we were both in high school that we began to form a friendship.

I thought she was beautiful. She had long blond hair, bright blue eyes, and an amazing smile. It was worth going to church just to see her! Her character was as beautiful as her appearance. She was always well-behaved. She was active in the youth group, always willing to help with the projects they performed. She would often go with her mother to visit the sick and aged, those no longer able to attend church. She was known in the church as a fine young Christian girl.

Her experience in visiting the sick and aged contributed to her decision to train as a nurse. Knowing that she was called to serve on the mission field, she recognized that she would need some type of specialized training. Nursing and education were the only viable options in those days, and she chose nursing. While still in high school, she began working on weekends in nursing homes. She knew the experience would increase her ability to be a good nurse and to care for her patients skillfully.

She assumed that at some point God would send her a husband who was also headed to the mission field. Many boys in high school showed interest in her, but she was very selective in choosing her friends. She was not interested in friendships with or dating unbelievers. She knew she was going to the mission field and did not want to waste time with boys who did not share her life goals and vision.

She did not want to be my friend. She was always polite, kind, and friendly to me. She even went to a few basketball games with me, but that was the end of it. She knew my reputation. After attending a few basketball games together, she knew the reputation was well deserved. I was a liar and a thief. She made it very clear she was only interested in Christian boys. She was friendly in the youth group, but she wanted nothing more to do with me.

I was disappointed. I was very interested in her, but she refused all future attempts to be part of her life. So when God told me that she would be my wife, I was extremely surprised. I liked the idea, but it did not seem possible. I knew only God could make that happen.

Immediately after my conversion, my conduct changed. I stopped stealing. I stopped lying. There was far less reason to lie since I was not stealing things. My language changed, too. I stopped using the coarse, crude, and vile language common to my peers at school.

Before long, people began to notice the change. The youth sponsors and the Sunday school teachers noticed a change in my attitude, also. The whole church had witnessed my conversion, and all were waiting to see if it was real. Carolyn noticed, too, but she did not say anything.

About the time of my confrontation with my philosophy lecturer, the Harvester Church youth group experienced a spiritual awakening. The Holy Spirit moved among us, and several expressed a desire for more and deeper spiritual teaching than we were getting in the youth group or in Sunday school. I thought a midweek Bible study for the high school and college age youth was needed. I knew no one at church would accept the idea if I suggested it, so I presented the idea to Pete, the leader of our youth group.

Pete was a fine Christian youth. His father was a lecturer at Fort Wayne Bible College, and his older brother was attending seminary. Everyone expected Pete to attend seminary and train for pastoral ministry, too. Pete was known and respected for his Christian reputation and behavior.

I presented a plan to Pete. Interested youth would meet in various members' homes. Pete and I would take turns leading the Bible study. Pete would be "in charge," and if we had any serious Bible problems we would discuss them with his father and then share our findings with the group. Pete agreed to present this plan to the pastor, seeking his approval for the activity. When Pete went to meet with the pastor, I waited in the foyer outside the pastor's office. My reputation was not one that would have encouraged the pastor to approve our request. Pete, though, was able to secure his approval.

With pastoral approval, Pete and I began recruiting others to attend. Our biggest problem was transportation. There was no night-time public transportation in our town. The youth needed their parents to take them by car to their events. Some parents were eager to do so, knowing that a Bible study was a far better activity than what most young people were doing at that time. Many of the youth, though, would not have a ride to the meeting place. Since I had a driver's license and a car, I was available to pick up other youth and take them to the meeting. I would also take them home. One of the youth needing a ride was Carolyn.

Carolyn was always the first person I picked up before the Bible study and the last person I took home. It gave me time to talk with her personally. She was nervous at first but gradually began to trust me. She listened to my teaching in the Bible study and observed my interaction with Pete when there was disagreement about the meaning of a text. She watched how I responded to other members who disagreed with me or who asked for further information. She recognized that I knew the Bible well, and that I was able to research a passage, gain an understanding of it, and explain it so others could understand it. She grew in Christ as a result of my teaching, as did others. When the academic year ended, so did our Bible study. During the summer months, all would have various family activities so it was impossible to continue to meet during our summer vacation. Carolyn and I began dating regularly.

After graduating from high school, I began working at a local factory. My hours were 3:18 to 11:48 p.m., Monday through Friday. But Saturday night was time for Carolyn! I worked hard in the factory, but I worked just as hard to find something to do every Saturday night that would interest Carolyn. We went to ball games. We went to concerts in the park. We want to anything I could find that would interest her. Every Saturday night we were together. We were also together at church every Sunday morning and Sunday evening. After church we would join others from the church for hamburgers, fries, and a Coke (or Pepsi). Love began to grow.

At the end of the summer we both enrolled in Fort Wayne Bible College. We were both in the missions training program, so we would be in many of the same courses. I was looking forward to continuing our relationship as we prepared for missionary service. Carolyn, though, had a different idea. She wanted to stop dating when we began classes. She wanted to meet other guys. She wanted to date other guys. She wanted me to stay away from her after classes began. If we were seen together regularly, other guys would assume we were in a serious relationship and not ask her out.

I told Carolyn I understood her point. I did not agree with it, but I understood. I did not like the idea, but if that was what she wanted I would comply with her wishes.

When classes began, we met frequently. We had many of the same classes. Since I had learned so much of the Bible at church, the Bible courses were easy for me, especially in the first year. Carolyn had a little more difficulty with the classes than me, so it was natural that I offered to help her study—in the library, of course. I got to meet her roommate in the college dorm. I got to meet the girls who became her friends. We were all in our first year of Bible college, so it was natural that we would hang out together during the school day. I was still working the same hours at the factory, so Carolyn was free in the evenings to develop other friendships.

At church, we were still good friends. We worked together with the high school youth group, and we participated in the college youth group activities. We still often had hamburgers, fries, and a Coke on Sunday evenings. But she was dating other guys. She wanted to know who God had chosen for her life partner.

In January she baked me a birthday cake. She and her roommate presented it to me after class, and Carolyn insisted her roommate take a photograph of us together. By February we were studying together in the library every day after lunch. I had to complete my study assignments before I went to work at the factory, but I always had time to help her with her Bible courses. She was dating one other guy now.

By March we were talking about missionary service. She would begin her nursing training in the next semester. She would have to transfer to a local nursing college, but I would continue at Fort Wayne Bible College. The nursing school enrolled only women students, so I found that encouraging. I was also encouraged to learn that she was no longer dating other guys.

In April, while we were working on her history of missions assignment in the library, I asked her to marry me. She wanted to know how that would work since we were both still in college. I explained that we would determine a wedding date later, probably a date after we completed our training. But I was working in the factory and could afford to provide a home for us, pay our college bills, and complete our training as a married couple if we chose to do so. No matter when we were married, we would serve God as missionaries wherever he sent us.

It was time for Carolyn's last class of the day, and I had to go to work. We gathered up our books, and I walked with her to her classroom. She did not say anything as we walked. Outside the door of the classroom she turned to look at me and said, "Yes, Wayne, I will marry you." She went into class, and I went to work.

She told me later that when she sat down at her desk in class, a friend looked at her and took note of her huge smile and flushed face. Her friend asked, "What happened to you? Did he ask you to marry him?" It was April 1971.

Over a year later, as we were making plans for our wedding, Carolyn asked me why I was so calm when she told me she wanted to date other guys. She said it surprised her that I did not object or get angry about it. Then, when she was dating other guys, I never made any problems for her. It was not the reaction she expected. She wanted me to explain it to her. She just did not understand.

I explained that I wanted her to marry me because she knew I was the man God had chosen for her and because she knew I loved her. I did not want her to marry me because she was afraid of what would happen if she rejected me.

"Besides," I said, "I knew you would come back."

"How did you know that?" she asked.

"Well, God told me you would be my wife," I replied.

"When did He tell you that?" she asked incredulously.

"On the day I was converted." I said with a smile. Then I told her for the first time the complete story of what God told me that night. I had told her about God warning me it was the last time He would call me. I had told her that God said I was to attend Fort Wayne Bible College and become a missionary, a prophet to the nations. But I had not told her that God said I would marry her. Now, I told her I knew she would come back to me and marry me because God had told me three years before that this would happen.

We were married on December 23,1972, after about an eighteen-month engagement. The second sign was now fulfilled.

Wedding Day

Give Me This Mountain

After Carolyn graduated from her nursing training and passed her state qualification exams, she began to work as a registered nurse (RN). I quit my job at the factory, so I could complete my training in one final year. Carolyn was at home with our son during the day while I was in class. I was home in the evenings with our son, completing my study assignments while Carolyn worked. I was also serving as a youth pastor and driving a school bus to earn extra income, but our goal was for me to complete my BA degree quickly, so we could move forward with our plans for missionary service.

As the end of the academic year and my graduation approached, we began to think seriously about where we would serve as missionaries. Neither Carolyn nor I had any specific plans. We were waiting for God to make His will known to us. We prayed for guidance and waited.

One day Rev. Joseph Conley came to speak in the college chapel service. Rev. Conley was the Executive Director of the Regions Beyond Missionary Union (RBMU). He had served this organization in Peru before assuming the task of directing its American branch. I had never heard of RBMU or of Rev. Conley. He was just another missions speaker in the college chapel. Chapel attendance was mandatory, but I was always interested in hearing missionary speakers, so I was eager to hear him speak.

Conley spoke from Joshua 14. He reviewed the story of Caleb standing before Joshua, reminding Joshua of the promise Moses had made to Caleb. Moses had promised that Caleb would receive the land he had scouted when he was sent as one of the twelve to scout the land they were to conquer. Caleb stood before Joshua as the land was apportioned to the tribe of Judah and said, "Give me this mountain!" Conley challenged us to ask God for a mountain to conquer for His glory.

It was a powerful challenge. I wanted to claim my mountain, but I just did not know where it was located. Did God have one for me? After exegeting the text Conley presented a ministry need, a mountain that needed to be conquered. He told us about the movement of the Holy Spirit among the Dayak people of West Kalimantan, Indonesia. I had heard of the Dayaks and of Borneo; but I had never heard of Kalimantan or of Indonesia. Conley, by the working of the Holy Spirit, had my full attention.

Conley read a letter he had recently received from one of his missionary staff who was working in West Kalimantan with the Dayaks. The letter was written by a Dayak village headman to the RBMU staff member, who had sent it on to Conley. The headman stated that his village had recently heard about Jesus Christ. Someone had visited the village to tell them about Jesus and then moved on to another village. Now, they wanted to become Christians, but they did not know how. So the headman had one request, "Can you send someone to teach us to be Christians?"

"Well, I can do that!" I thought. "They just need someone to teach them how to live for Jesus, to be His disciples. I have been doing that since I started that Bible study for my friends at Harvester."

After chapel I went to the library to find out where West Kalimantan was located and learn about the Dayaks. I read through several encyclopedias, learning all I could about this mountain that I was convinced

God was calling me to claim. The last entry I was able to read before I had to go to class contained a description of Pontianak, the provincial capital. It concluded, as I recall, by saying that because of its very high humidity and temperatures, "on any given day it can be the most miserable place on the face of the earth."

After classes were completed for the day I hurried home to share this with Carolyn. Rushing through the door of our apartment, I excitedly announced to Carolyn,

"I know where God wants us to go!"

"Where?" she asked.

"West Kalimantan, Indonesia!" I replied with unabated excitement.

"Where is that?" she asked in confusion. "I've never heard of it."

So began our education and preparation for ministry with the Dayaks in West Kalimantan, Indonesia. I was ordained to the Christian ministry on December 4, 1977 at Harvester Avenue Missionary Church. We left Fort Wayne for Indonesia nineteen days later, on December 23, 1977.

Departing for Indonesia.

Ministry Areas of West Kalimantan

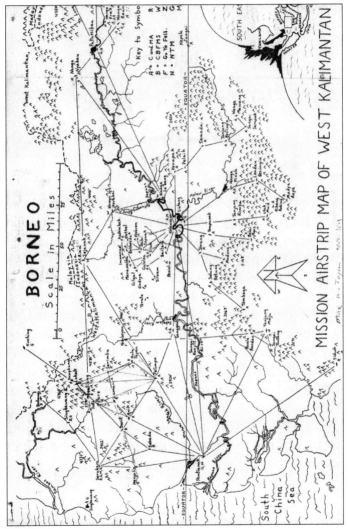

Ministry Areas of West Kalimantan

Chapter 2

WHY AM I HERE?

B y 1979 I had completed my training at Fort Wayne
Bible College. I had married the woman God
appointed for me, and we had two children, Joshua and
Rachel. We moved to Indonesia in January 1978. We
studied Indonesian language and culture at a school in
Bandung, West Java, for nine months.

We then moved to Ansang, West Kalimantan. In
Ansang was Berea Bible School, which was operated by
my mission team. It was my intent and expectation that I
would teach at the Bible school as soon as my language
was good enough to communicate well. However, after
only three months at Ansang, the mission team assigned
me to serve as district pastor in Menjalin, a neighboring
district. Since this was my assignment, I arranged to
move my family there in January 1979.

The Family in Bandung 1978.

The Beginning

Previous workers with my mission team, Rev. and Mrs. Henry Thiessen, had launched a good work in the Menjalin area. A mission house was built on land purchased by the mission but was to become church property. The Thiessens had also constructed an airstrip which enabled the Mission Aviation Fellowship (MAF) planes to assist them in their ministry. Planes could land on the airstrip to bring in needed supplies and mail. Planes could also pick up Henry for travel to more remote areas where there was no resident minister of the gospel or evangelist.

Henry was known throughout the district as a powerful evangelist. He loved trekking out to the remotest villages in the district to preach the gospel. He was an excellent volleyball player, which made him very popular with the young men in the villages. He was fluent in Bahasa Bekua, the local Dayak dialect, too. His enthusiasm, volleyball skills, and use of Bahasa Bekua opened the doors of every village in the district to hear the gospel. God blessed his ministry so that by the time I moved to Menjalin, there were twelve established churches, with their own buildings, in the district.

The Mission Team

In another two dozen villages, believers would gather for worship and teaching whenever Henry or one of the *guru Injil* (teachers of the gospel), who worked with Henry, would visit the village. These village ministries were called preaching points.

My assignment in Menjalin was to oversee the ministry of a dozen churches, two dozen preaching points, and the work of eight Dayak men who served as *guru Injil* in the district. It was a big task, and a heavy responsibility. It was made even more challenging by my youth and inexperience.

I had graduated from Bible college only four years before. I had only one year of full-time church ministry experience, and that had been in the United States. I had only nine months of Indonesian language training and three months experience with Dayak culture, which had significant differences from the Indonesian culture I had learned in Bandung. In addition, my family and I had to learn to live without electricity, to cook over a wood-burning stove, to bathe in the river, to obtain our food supplies without a local grocery store we could visit at need. I also had to learn to use a motorcycle as the primary means of transportation for my family of four. More importantly, I had to learn how to minister to Dayaks and in Dayak churches. I had to learn to understand Dayak culture, Dayak thought, Dayak history, hopes, dreams, and fears. I had many lessons to learn before I could be an effective missionary.

It was a struggle. Everything was different from what I had known in the United States. The weather was different. It seemed it would never stop raining. And the heat was unbelievable! Every day, the sun would rise in the clear blue sky to drive away the welcomed coolness of the jungle night. The merciless heat would grow to levels I had never experienced in the United States. But as a hard-working American, I was not about to let the heat stop me from completing my assigned tasks. There was work to be done, and I was going to do it— no matter how hot the sun nor how much in rained!

The Power of the Sun

I would work in my office during the day. I would study the Scriptures, so I had a biblical message to preach during the week. I would study the Indonesian language, searching the Indonesian dictionary for the new vocabulary I needed to express the biblical truths. I studied hard every day until noon. My knowledge of Scripture increased. My ability in the Indonesian language increased. My understanding of Dayak culture increased as I ministered in the villages, talked with the believers, and interacted with unbelievers. So, the mornings were always devoted to study in the office.

The afternoons were devoted to work on the house and grounds. The mission house needed extensive repairs, and I had to do them myself. I put my hammer and saw to good use. I repaired the holes in the floor and sealed up the leaks where the endless rain came in through the roof. I repaired the troughs that brought rainwater into the kitchen and bathroom. I repaired the screen on the doors to reduce the number of mosquitoes in the house, in hopes that we could avoid bouts with malaria and dengue fever. I repaired the clothesline poles so Carolyn would have a place to hang the laundry to dry. I repaired the electrical wiring in the house and the garage. I set up our generator, so we could have electricity in the evenings. The electric lights, the music from the cassette player, and the coolness of the electric fans were welcome relief for Carolyn and the kids. Carolyn especially appreciated the bright lights since I was away preaching in the villages most nights. She, too, was struggling to adapt to the new environment. The lights helped her to feel safe when I was not there.

Almost daily the grass around the house needed to be cut. I could not afford to pay a local man to cut the grass, so I had to do it myself. Unable to afford the power tools I used in the United States, I learned to cut grass with an old-fashioned double-edged grass cutter. I wanted my children to have a place to play, to run and jump, and to make friends with the local village children, so the grass had to be cut. I wanted to keep the snakes and scorpions out of my house, so the grass had to be cut. Rain or shine, I had to cut the grass.

So it was that one day while I was cutting the grass, I discovered I was cold. Yes, cold. I was so cold that I was shivering. It made no sense. I was standing in the yard under the bright tropical sun without a cloud in the sky. The sun was fiercely hot, and perspiration was streaming down my back and arms like water down the Manyuke River. How could I be cold?

Confused, I returned to the house and asked my wife, who is a registered nurse, "What does it mean when I am standing in the tropical sun and shivering from cold?"

"Oooh, Wayne!" she exclaimed! "It means you have heat stroke! If we don't get you cooled off immediately, you will be dead before the sun goes down!"

It was the first of many times this dear woman whom God gave me as a partner in ministry saved my life. Soon I was sitting in a tank of cold water, drinking sweet ice tea with lemon, with a fan (Yes, Carolyn fired up the generator in the middle of the day!) blowing its cold breeze directly on my face. Every minute or two Carolyn would pour a dipper of cold water over my head (I think she enjoyed doing that!) to continue reducing the heat in my head and lower my body temperature.

It took me two days to recover my strength. When I returned to cutting the grass in the sun, I wore a bamboo hat given me by a *guru Injil* who had learned of my illness and took pity on my ignorance. He explained, "The tropical sun is too strong for anyone to work out there without a hat, Pak Pendeta. (Pak Pendeta was what the Dayaks called ordained men.)You must learn from us how to work in the fields. Wear this hat when you cut the grass."

I listened. I learned; but I had so much to learn. I had learned the power of the sun, but I had not learned the power of the rain.

The Power of the Rain

A song my wife and I loved to hear when we were dating contains this line: "It don't rain in Indianapolis in the summer time." In Indiana we get twelve to eighteen inches of rain every year. The months of July and August are very dry. Very little rain falls "in the summertime" in our state capital, Indianapolis. As I prepared to move to Indonesia, I studied the climate of West Kalimantan. The texts I read indicated that average rainfall in West Kalimantan was 120–180 inches per year—ten times what I was used to in Indiana!

While growing up in Indiana I learned from my father that rain was never an excuse for not going to church. During my childhood, we lived only a short distance from our church building. Often, on warm summer nights, my brother and I would walk to church for the training hour. Our parents would come later in the car. Rain was never a problem. I could carry an umbrella if the rain was light. If it was a heavy rain, Dad would take us in the car. Rain was not a problem, and it was never an excuse for not going to church!

So, when I began my Menjalin ministry I held to the same principle. Rain was not an excuse for not going to church. Even though I had to travel by motorcycle, rain was not an acceptable excuse for missing church.

My regular ministry plan was for me to visit an established church every Sunday. I would visit with the local pastor. We would discuss the ministry in the village. I would ask about the local leaders, about the Sunday school, about the youth, and about the prayer meetings. I would ask about what he was doing to open ministry in near-by villages. I would ask about his preaching schedule and topics about which he was preaching. I would encourage him in his work, offer some suggestions as led by the Spirit, deliver the morning message, visit in some of the believers' homes, and then leave for the village I would serve in the evening.

During the week I would visit some of the preaching points in the district. Tuesday, Wednesday, and Thursday nights, I would visit a different village preaching point. Sometimes I would take a *guru Injil* with me, but most of the time I would go alone. Most of the time, I had to travel in the rain. While it may not rain in Indianapolis in the summertime, it seemed to me that it never stopped raining in West Kalimantan— no matter what the season. It seemed to me that West Kalimantan had only two seasons, the rainy season and the rainier season. It just never seemed to stop raining.

Of course, it always started to rain just as I was leaving for the village I intended to visit. The sky would darken with clouds, a bolt or two of lightening would flash, and then the rain would come, pummeling on my helmet and coat like a thousand drumsticks beating out an angry rhythm designed to persuade me to stay home. It seemed that each raindrop was screaming the Devils' message, "Stay home! It's too dangerous! The trail is long and dark! It is slick, and you will slide off the mountainside into the swamp and jungle below! It is too dangerous to go tonight! Stay home with your wife and children. Enjoy the warmth of your house. Have a cup of *teh susu* (strong tea mixed with sweetened condensed milk) and play a game with your children. Spend the evening with your wife. You can't go tonight! It's raining!"

I had been trained well, though. I knew rain was never an excuse to miss church services. I mounted my Suzuki 125cc trail bike and hit the road! Rain or shine, I was going to preach the gospel in the village. I had promised them I was coming, and I would not break my promise! I had much to learn about the power of the rain in West Kalimantan.

When it rains in West Kalimantan, the mountain trails become mountain rivers. The rainwater rushes down the hillsides, through the dry-rice fields and rubber gardens, until it finds its way to the trail. Then it follows that trail down the mountainside to the river. Water flowed in a mighty steam down the mountainside, taking with it leaves in abundance, loose boards, cast-off coconut shells, and small branches. It undermines the soil around the trees, sending them crashing down on the trail. Often I had to stop in the middle of the rainstorm, pull out my machete, and cut a way over, under, around, or though the barrier! I was going to the village and no little rainstorm was going to stop me! The gospel had to be preached!

More than once I fell and slid down the mountain-side while sitting atop my Suzuki. More than once I could not get traction in the mud and slid back down the trail, with my tire spewing up a mighty spray of muddy water as I revved up the engine. More than once I arrived at the village covered in mud, leaves, and debris from the jungle. More than once I arrived with bleeding cuts, torn pants, ripped shirts, and a dam-aged Suzuki—but I preached the gospel! I was proud that the rain never stopped me. One day, though, a dear Dayak brother explained to me how my actions were endangering my Dayak friends.

This brother in Christ, Yahya by name, spoke as plainly to me as did my friend who gave me a hat to wear in the sun. Yahya told me it was easy for me to travel in the rain. I had a good rain suit, and tough rubber boots. I could ride a motorcycle in the rain and stay relatively dry. My hands and face would get wet, but most of my body would stay dry and warm. It is not so for the Dayaks. They do not have raincoats that shed the water. When they walk from their houses to the church for the meeting, they get completely soaked. Then they have to sit in the church service in their wet clothes. They get cold. Then they have to walk home in the rain—getting wet again just as they are beginning to get dry! They arrive home cold and wet, and then try to sleep. The next morning, they are sick.

"The cold and wet does not trouble you," Yayha told me, "as it does the Dayaks in the villages. You are used to colder weather in the United States. You welcome the rain as it cools the temperature and refreshes you from the heat. You can go home and change clothes, have a cup of hot tea or coffee or chocolate, and get warm before you go to bed. Our Dayak believers cannot do that. They do not have extra clothes or money for extra tea or coffee in the middle of the night."

"Further," he explained, "if you fall and get hurt, your wife has medicines at home she can use to help you. You have aspirin for pain and antibiotics for infections. You have sulfa drugs for an upset stomach, and daraprim for malaria. Your wife can sew up any bad cuts you get. She has the tools you need to do this and the skill to do it. If you are seriously hurt, you can call the MAF plane to come get you and take you to the hospital. You can afford to pay for the travel and the doctors and the medicines. Our Dayak brothers cannot do this. They do not have the skill, the tools, the medicines, or the money."

"Pak Pendeta," Yahya said sternly, "when it rains at time to go to church, please stay home. When you go, you force our Dayak believers to go out in the rain. You force them to risk their health, their safety, and their prosperity for a church service. If you do not go that night, you can go another night. God knows your heart. He will understand you were willing to go, but you stayed home for the health and safety of these people. Please, Pak Pendata, don't put the health and safety of our people at risk on a rainy night."

I listened to Yahya. I learned from him. I had greater lessons to learn, though, that only God Himself could teach me.

The Power of God's Call

The greatest and most important lesson I had to learn was why I was in West Kalimantan. The importance of this lesson was driven powerfully into my thinking during the celebration of Good Friday and Easter in 1979.

As *Pendeta Daerah* (District Ordained Minister), I was the only one authorized by the national church to baptize believers in the Menjalin district. Several churches had new believers who wanted to be baptized, and all were waiting for me to visit their church to do the baptisms. Thus, I agreed to celebrate Good Friday at the church pastored by Alekandar and his wife Gemitir.

The Allen Family, Easter 1979

Alek, as he was commonly called, and Gemitir had one child, a daughter; but Gemitir was well advanced toward the time of giving birth to her second child. The district leadership had decided that Alek and Gemitir should be moved from the very remote village church they served to pastor one of the larger churches of the district on the main road. This would also make it easier for Gemitir to have the medical help she would need when her child was born.

Our plan was for me to preach at Alek's church, baptize the new believers, and then transport Gemitir and her daughter on my motorcycle back to the Menjalin community. Alek would follow with all their earthly possessions packed on the back of his bicycle. They would live in Menjalin with relatives until the new child was strong, and then they would move to the new assignment. In the meantime, Alek would commute to the new assignment by bicycle or public transport. It was a good plan, and I looked forward eagerly to this ministry trip.

As I considered the distances and travel time involved, I concluded that it would be best for me to travel to another mission station on the night before Good Friday. I would have opportunity to fellowship with another missionary. We could pray together, read the Scriptures together, and I could ask him about various aspects of ministry in West Kalimantan. He was born in West Kalimantan to missionary parents. He spoke Bekua and Banana, two Dayak dialects, fluently. He knew the Dayak worldview far better than I. Spending Thursday night with him would be a good time for learning, for fellowship, and for mutual encouragement in the Lord. I sent word ahead to him, and he was expecting my arrival. We were both looking forward to a quiet evening together before the heavy weekend ministries to come.

The trip started smoothly. It had not rained for two days (praise God!), so the mountain trail was dry and easy to manage. One unique thing happened on the way through the jungle to the paved road leading to Ansang in the Menyuke River valley. Near the village of Ladangan, I came to a village-style bridge over a deep chasm containing a small mountain stream. When the rains came, this little stream would swell up into a ten-foot rushing torrent, but now it was a tame little thing. The bridge had been constructed by felling two trees, each about a foot in diameter, across the chasm. The bark had not been removed from the tree trunks, nor had the trunks been squared by saw or axe. The round tree trunks were just placed across the chasm and boards nailed to them. However, most of the boards had vanished (probably taken away by villagers who needed to repair holes in the floor of their houses). All that remained were the two tree trunks laying across the chasm.

If I had been walking, crossing over would not have been a problem. Walking on a fallen tree was a skill I had learned as a boy when visiting my grandparents' farms back in Tennessee. Here, though, I had a motorcycle to get across this ten-foot chasm. Well, being young and foolish, and inexperienced with a motorcycle, I lined the tires up with the tree and drove the bike across the chasm on the tree trunk. No problem. I was across and went on my way.

Trouble began when I reached the paved road leading to my friend's house. The Snowy Mountain Engineering Company's road crew had torn up the paved road. They were working under a contract from the United Nations to put a paved road through the Manyuke Valley to connect that region with the provincial capital, Pontianak, and the next administrative district in Sanggau. The red clay placed as a foundation for the improved road made it impossible for me to reach my friend's house. It was too late in the day to return to my home, or even to go to the church where I was to minister the next morning. I decided to spend the night in Ansang, on the Bible school campus.

The next morning I started back to the village where I was to meet Alek and Gemitir. In my frustration and disappointment, I did not consider how the rain that fell that night would affect the trail.

Soon I came to the bridge over the chasm. It was the same bridge as the day before. There were no boards on the tree trunks, but I had ridden my bike over it yesterday, so it would be no problem to do it again. I lined up the tires with the tree trunk and started across.

My front tire had already reached the other side when I felt the back tire slide to the left, toward the space between the two trees that formed the bridge. I fell backward between the two tree trunks. In desperation, hoping to avoid falling the twenty feet to the rocky stream bed below, which I knew was filled with sharp broken tree fragments washed down from the mountains, I threw an arm and a leg across each tree. The motorcycle continued to fall slowly backward until its steering bar was resting on my waist. I was hanging from the tree trunks, holding on with an arm and a leg across each tree.

The 125cc Suzuki trail bike was hanging from my waist. If I released an arm to try to move the bike, the bike and I both would fall into the chasm. There was nothing I could do except hang there and wait for help. I called for help. I screamed with all my might. I called until I was hoarse—until I could scream no more. No one came. Then I began to talk to God.

I was mad! I was mad at God! Angry questions and thoughts filled my mind. What am I doing here! Why did you bring me here? I could be at home in my own town, pastoring a local church. I could work from a nice office and lead the worship services and minister to the people of God in my own country and in my own language. I could serve where I understood what people were doing and why they did things. I could drive a car, not a motorcycle. I could stay dry when I traveled. I could preach on Sunday and visit those in jail, feed the poor, and pray for those in the hospital!

"Why God?" I screamed. "Why do I have to be here? If I pastored a church in the United States I could visit my father and mother on Saturday. I could take my children to meet their grandparents! I could eat my favorite foods and still lead a church of your people! Why God? Why did I have to leave my home, my parents, and my people to come out here to suffer heat stroke, slide down mountainsides, and fall off broken bridges into raging rivers!

The heavens were sealed up like a gasoline drum. There was no answer. No vision. No response. No word of comfort or solace—just the echoes of my own voice as I screamed out my anger and frustration to God.

Eventually, God sent someone to help me. When I saw my rescuers, I began to laugh. I needed a couple of strong Dayak men to lift the motorcycle up onto the road. Instead God sent me a little boy, about nine years old, and his grandmother, who looked to be about ninety! Seeing my situation, they both began to laugh, too.

Together we tried to get that motorcycle back on the road. We failed. The motorcycle fell into the chasm, which was now flooded from the previous night's rain. I dropped into the water and moved the motorcycle to the shallow water at the edge of the chasm. With the help of my two rescuers, I soon had the motorcycle back on the road.

Just as we completed the task, a huge group of people arrived from the village of Ladangan. Apparently news of my trouble had reached the village, and everyone came to see what kind of silly thing the foreigner had done this time. The crowd happily escorted me back to the village and watched as I worked on the engine.

I was unable to complete my scheduled ministry for Good Friday and Easter Sunday. I spent Friday trying to get the motorcycle engine repaired. When I could not get it started, I returned to the Bible school campus to spend the night. With help from the Bible school maintenance man, I was able to continue my journey on Saturday afternoon.

Gemitir, Alekandar's wife, was anxiously awaiting my arrival. They had heard from other travelers of my fall on the bridge, so they had completed the Good Friday services without me. Alekandar preached and performed the baptisms without me. On Saturday morning they were packed and ready to move to Menjalin. Trusting that I would arrive soon, Alekandar loaded up all their earthly possessions on their bicycle and departed for his new home. Gemitir, seven months pregnant, and her two-year-old daughter waited for me.

However, as I approached Karangan I learned that the Mempawah River had flooded the town. It was impossible to get the motorcycle into town due to floodwaters. The water was so deep the Dayaks, most of whom were barely 5'0" tall, could not pass. It was impossible, too, for Gemitir, in her condition and carrying an infant to attempt any further travel. It was also impossible to return to Gemitir's home. All their goods were on the way to Menjalin. There was no food or other necessities at their old home. She was adamant that we could not return to the church village.

We considered many options. I even recruited the local police to assist transporting Gemitir on a home-made raft to a safe place in town, but Gemitir was not willing to risk that option. In the end, Gemitir found a family member living near the trail and opted to remain there until the waters receded.

Anxious to reach Menjalin for Easter services, I left the motorcycle in the care of Gemitir and the local police. I walked through floodwaters up to my shoulders to reach the Karangan marketplace, where water was running up to my waist in the street. The Mempawah River ran through the middle of the town. The only bridge across the river was covered by the raging floodwaters. Only the tops of the railings on the sides of the bridge were visible, and the current was rushing by on its way to the South China Sea. Folks told me not to try it, but I would not listen. I was determined to reach Menjalin.

When I tried to cross, I was washed off the bridge by the force of the current. I was convinced that if I could just reach the railings on the bridge, I could pull myself across the part of the river where the current was too strong for me to stand. I tried a second time, but again I was washed off the bridge before I could reach the railings. At this point, an enterprising Dayak man arrived with a motorboat. He loaded the boat to the gunwales with people like me who wanted to reach the other side, and, for Rp.100 ($0.17) per person, ferried us all to the other side.

It was now late afternoon on Saturday as I began the long walk to Menjalin. The road, which ran beside the

Mempawah River, was flooded. The water was up to my waist most of the way, but it often rose to my neck. I grabbed two long bamboo poles from the flotsam on the water and used them to test my footing. I could not see the road, so I had no way of knowing where the ditches on each side of the road were under the water. I used the poles to test the ground in front of me before each step. After sundown it began to rain again. I was a blind man feeling my way in the darkness. Foolishly, opting to travel light on the walk to Menjalin, I had left my flashlight in my backpack with my motorcycle.

It is only a bit over six miles from Karangan to Menjalin. On a good day I could run it in an hour. No problem, even with a small backpack. But in the darkness, and testing the ground with my poles before every step, with the floodwater above my waist, it was slow traveling—very, very slow.

I was tired. I had not eaten since I left the Bible school campus that morning. I had not had anything to drink, either. I knew every coffee shop between Menjalin and Karangan. They were regular stops for me. Now, there was nothing before me but the black night. No lights glimmered in the darkness promising hot coffee, fried bananas, or *martabak* (a crispy dough wrapped around a savory egg or sweet peanut filling, called peanut pancake in Singapore). There was not even a place to sit down and rest. There was only the blackness of night, the falling rain, the cold water, and the search for a safe place for my next step.

Suddenly the jungle silence was broken by the sound of voices approaching from the direction of Menjalin. I was too tired to greet them, but when the beam of their flashlight revealed my presence, they were astonished to see a foreigner walking the dark, flooded trail.

"Where are you going?" In their surprise they used their local dialect. Happily, it was one of the few dialect questions I understood.

"Going home to Menjalin." I replied in Indonesian.

"Impossible, Pak Pendeta! You can't get there! The flood waters are deeper there than here! There is no way to get across the river! You can't even see the bridge!

Recognizing that I did not understand their dialect, the speaker answered in Indonesian.

"What else can I do? I have no other option. There is no place to stop." I replied.

"Come with us!" they replied. "There is a place close by to spend the night."

I did not hesitate. I threw away my bamboo poles and followed them as they found a trail leading up to higher ground. After a short walk, no more than a half-mile, we came to a small village. Kerosene lanterns illuminated the small shop that served as a convenient place for folks to gather and talk about the flood. My guides were greeted like old friends, and they quickly explained my situation.

Someone handed me a towel to dry my face. Someone else put a cup of hot coffee in my hand and guided me to a stool, so I could sit down. A woman handed me a sarong and told me to give her my clothes. Seeing the confusion and embarrassment in my face, a man stopped laughing long enough to explain that I was to wear the sarong while the lady dried my clothes over the fire. Thankfully, I had learned how to remove my clothes under the sarong so my clothes soon disappeared into the back of the store.

The lady returned with a heaping plate of steaming rice topped by a fried egg and boiled cassava leaves. This was followed by another cup of hot coffee.

This was when I noticed that the group who brought me to this place was not to be seen. I asked where they were, and learned that they had left, continuing their journey to their own destinations. These wonderful folks had seen my condition, taken me to a place of safety, introduced me to the local residents, and then continued their journey. I never did find out their names or where they lived.

A few minutes later, the lady returned my clothes, dry and warm from the fire—which helped me to stop shivering. When I was dressed, a man told me to follow him. Without question or hesitation, I followed him into the darkness outside the shop. He led the way through the village to a large board house. I followed him up the steps and into the front room. He showed me a full-sized bed complete with a mattress, a blanket, and a mosquito net.

"Sleep well," he said as he turned and walked out the door into the night. I did. I slept as only the truly exhausted can sleep.

When I woke, the sun was shining in through the open door. As I walked out onto the veranda, a man greeted me and then led me up the path to the store where I had eaten the night before. I was greeted with hearty amusement and good will. Hot coffee was followed by another plate of steaming rice with scrambled eggs and cassava leaves. I chatted with the men as I ate, but most of the conversation was in dialect between the men themselves. Clearly, they were still amused by my plight. I knew my story would now become legend in the district. These folks were having a good time laughing about it, and the story would be retold for weeks to come!

Soon I was ready to resume my journey to Menjalin. I inquired about what I owed them for the meals, the coffee, and the place to sleep. They refused any payment. I offered a gift for their children, to help with their school expenses, as an expression of my gratitude. These wonderfully kind, hospitable, and generous Dayaks refused to accept anything more than my thanks and my prayer of blessing. So I took the path back to the river and continued my journey.

I searched for them in the weeks that followed. I drove the road many times, and every time I searched for the path that I followed that night. I asked at the local shops and a few of the houses on the road. No one could point me to the village where I was warmed, refreshed, fed, and given refuge from the floodwaters. I hope to meet them in heaven. They were God's angels for me that night.

The floodwaters were still chest-deep on the road, but at least I could see where I was going. I still needed a pole to test my footing, but I could travel much faster now. The water was cool. The sun was hot. Swift was the journey.

At Menjalin the waters had receded sufficiently that I could see the bridge as I approached the market place. I created quite a stir as I walked through the market place with water now only up to my thighs. Folks greeted me from the porches that were above the floodwaters. It seemed the story of my misfortunes had preceded me to town. Someone had seen me washed off the bridge in Karangan but had not seen me make my way back to solid ground. Apparently, there was some discussion of how far downriver my body would be found. As I reached the south end of town I emerged from the floodwaters onto dry ground. The last mile to the mission station was an easy walk, but it was with great relief that I walked up onto the porch outside the front door of my home.

Tired and filthy, I sat down on the bench beside the door. I looked down the airstrip to the church. As I sat there, folks began to exit the church. Easter services were complete. After greeting the congregation as they departed, Carolyn and our children started up to the house.

The children saw me first and broke into a run, each eager to be the first to welcome me home. Their laughter and excitement to see me was a welcomed encouragement. Carolyn greeted me with a smile and quiet words that masked her concern.

"We heard about the bridge in Karangan but nothing after that." she said. "Since you were not here, and he could not get back to Sompak, Alekandar preached. We prayed for you in church this morning. Glad you made it home."

I was glad I made it home, too. But as I sat there, trying to gather enough energy to do what needed to be done one question filled my mind—the one question that I screamed into the empty sky as I hung from the bridge with a motorcycle suspended by its handlebars from my waist.

What am I doing here?

Again, I prayed, "Lord, what am I doing *here?* Why did you send me here? I could serve you far better back in the United States. I know what to do there. Lord, *why did you send me here"* Still, there was no answer.

Chapter 3

A LIGHT TO THE NATIONS

After the disaster on the bridge near Ladangan on Good Friday, I returned to my assigned ministries in Menjalin with a heavy heart. I had called out to God, but He had not answered. This question burned in my mind as I went about my duties. I continued to preach the gospel in village and town. I continued to encourage my fellow ministers of the gospel. I continued to serve the Dayak church in any way I could, but I wanted an answer. Why had God sent me here to this place that was so difficult for me when I could have served Him just as well in my own country, in my own language, and near my father's house?

The Road to Pudak

The Christmas season came upon us. Once again, all the local churches were calling for me, their district pastor, to visit them to celebrate the birth of the Christ Child, to baptize the new believers, and to strengthen the faith of those who had long followed Jesus. The preaching points were also calling for me to visit them.

The demand was far greater than I could possibly manage alone, so I gathered my colleagues, my Dayak brothers who proclaimed the gospel of Jesus with me. We prepared a ministry schedule, so all could be served and all could hear the true story of the birth of the savior of the world. Since I had a motorcycle, and the others had to rely on bicycles and/or public transportation, I agreed to serve the most distant churches and preaching points. One of my assigned locations was to the church in the village of Pudak.

I had never been to Pudak. I had been to other churches and preaching points in that area, but for some reason I had never taken the road to Pudak, so I was eager to go. I knew it would be a long and difficult road, but time, distance, and difficulties had never stopped me before. I was determined to be in Pudak on December 27, 1979 to celebrate the birth of our Savior. However, knowing that it would be a challenging trip, I asked Joni to go with me. Joni was in his last year of high school and had worked with me in leading the youth group in Menjalin. He was a good lad, so I was very pleased he accepted my invitation to visit Pudak with me.

The day dawned bright and clear with a shining sun in a cloudless sky, but by midmorning the sun was hidden by black clouds, and the rain was pouring down like a waterfall. The rains continued all afternoon. Yahya advised me not to make the trip. My wife urged me not to go. I prayed for guidance. At five o'clock in the afternoon, just when I needed to start my journey, the rain stopped, the sky cleared, and the sun emerged. I believed that God had answered my prayers and opened the way for me to go. Joni and I mounted my 125cc Suzuki trail bike and hit the road for Pudak.

Dayak Village Church

We had to travel on an asphalt road for twelve miles before turning onto a jungle trail of red clay and large rocks. By the time I reached the turn, it was raining again—hard! Nonetheless, I pressed on for Pudak.

The road was filled with deep holes, and I had to weave between them to find solid ground. I had to go very slow, as each hole was filled with water and I had no idea of their depth. At one spot I had to put my foot into a hole to keep from falling to the ground. When I pulled my foot out of the mud at the bottom of the hole, my shoe stayed in the mud. (I never did find it and had to finish the trip with only one shoe.) Often, Joni had to walk on the side of the road while I maneuvered the Suzuki between the mud holes and over the rocks. Two hours later, at about seven o'clock, when we should have been at Pudak based on the normal travel time, we were only halfway there. We were tired, wet, and cold.

Pudak was still two hours away, and it was two hours back to Menjalin, too.

Wayne Returns from Village Ministry

I stopped at the home of another *guru Injil*, Nona Sar, who worked with us and pastored the village church in Sungai Pinggang. She refreshed us with hot tea and a dry seat on the porch. Joni and I discussed our plans with Nona Sar. Other believers in the village heard of our arrival and came to see what was happening. We talked at length about the road to Pudak. Was it flooded or was it passable? Was there a steep hill or mountain to climb? Was there a river to cross? Was there a swampy area that would be flooded so that we could not cross? Should we continue our trip or should we stop in Sungai Pinggang and celebrate Christmas with them?

No one present had been up the road to Pudak that day, but everyone declared it was impassable. We must not make the attempt, they said. It was too dangerous, they said. But no one would tell me about the hills or the rivers or the swamps. It seemed they were not actually talking to me about the road but just trying to persuade me to stay with them to celebrate Christmas at their church.

As we sat there on the porch deliberating what to do, I saw two men walking in the rain and coming from the direction of Pudak. I had met these men before in the nearby market town of Toho. They were schoolteachers from West Nusa Tenggara, a province on another Indonesian island. They had been assigned to teach in the government school in Pudak. They had just come from Pudak and affirmed to Joni and me that the road was passable. They had just walked the road and were sure that we could reach there without difficulty. They described the road for us, so we would not lose our way. They also affirmed that folks in Pudak were anxiously awaiting our arrival. I decided that we should press on. Looking back, I think I forgot to mention to them that Joni and I were traveling by motorcycle, not walking as they had done.

A Light in the Jungle

It was a dark, dark night. Heavy clouds hid the moon and stars. The rain continued to fall, sometimes heavy and sometimes light, but always enough to cloud our vision.

The West Nusa Tenggara teachers told me to take the first trail to the east after leaving Sungai Pinggang. I would have to cross a line of small hills, followed by a wide valley where some of the best rice paddies in the district were in constant cultivation thanks to the small river that flowed through the valley. Across the valley, up the hills on the far side, and down in the valley beyond I would find Pudak with lanterns blazing in the church and hot coffee to warm us.

There was boiled chicken and roasted pork waiting to be served up after the preaching, and *ketan* (a desert of sticky rice cooked in bamboo poles and spiced with garlic and coconut milk) without limit! It would be a great celebration and well worth the effort to get there!

Joni and I found the turn without difficulty. The trail over the hills was slippery, but I had no trouble getting traction to make the climb. The descent into the valley was exciting. I had to guard constantly against sliding off the trail and down the hillside. I had to keep my speed low, so I could make the sharp turns on the steep descent. But God was with us. We reached the paddy fields safely. Now things really got interesting.

As I looked across the valley that should have been filled with growing rice, with a river flowing quietly through the center, all I could see was a huge lake. There was nothing to be seen but water. Joni and I sat on my Suzuki and scanned carefully what we could see in the light of my motorcycle headlamp. All was water. We knew there had to be hills on the other side, but we could not see them in the darkness. We could see the glimmer of a path in front of my motorcycle tire, but it was under water. I could not tell if the water got deeper as the path went further into the valley. Finally, Joni tapped me on the shoulder and pointed ahead.

"Bapak," he said. "Look over there. It's a bridge. It must be the bridge over the river. Let's drive up to the bridge and then see what we need to do next."

It sounded like a good plan to me, so I put the bike in gear and headed out into the dark waters. The further I went the deeper the water became. I realized my Suzuki engine would be flooded by water unless I kept the RPM very high and plowed ahead. I opened the gas wide and with a great roar from the engine we sped ahead like a beam of light! I just wanted to get up on that bridge before the engine died. Then I could decide what to do next.

As soon as I hit the gas, Joni began to scream!

"Don't do that, Pak! Don't do that! Stop! Stop! It's dangerous, Pak! Stop! Stop!"

I didn't understand a word he said because, in his fear, he reverted to Bekua, his heart language. I was still struggling to master the Indonesian language, so I had not even begun to learn the local dialect. I determined just to get up onto that bridge, and then I would ask what he was yelling about. Bad idea!

As we approached the bridge, too late I realized there was a steep incline in the road leading up to the bridge — perfectly designed to launch a wheelie. As the front wheel rose into the air above the bridge, I threw my weight forward to drive the front tire down and prevent the bike flipping over backwards. Thankfully, the tire began to descend, and I knew we would not do a backflip.

Then I saw there were no planks on the bridge! There were only the studs that were to hold the boards in place — the boards were gone for at least six feet of the bridge. The front tire dropped into the gap and slammed into the first board.

Carried forward by the momentum of our speed, I was thrown over the handlebars and into the air! I flew through the air for several yards before I hit the water with a great splash. Going in headfirst as I did, I thoroughly expected I would hit the ground with my head, break my neck, and die in that Dayak rice paddy on my way to celebrate the coming to earth of the Prince of Peace. "Well," I thought, "It is a good way to die." But all I hit was water.

Eventually the water slowed my descent, and my body's natural buoyancy began to carry me back to the surface of the water. When I reached the surface, I took a deep breath and looked all around. There was only the darkness of a rainy night in the jungle. I could not see the rain hitting me in the face. I could not see my hands. I could not even see them when I wiped the grass from my face. It was total, absolute blackness. I had no idea where to go to get out of the water. I could swim, but I had no idea which way to go. If I chose wrong, I would be washed down river and drown. I was lost in total darkness with no idea where to go to find safety.

At that moment Joni turned on his flashlight. He was standing on the path leading away from the bridge. I do not know what happened to Joni. I only know that when Joni turned on that light I knew where to go to find safety, to get out of the water and back onto solid ground. I would have drowned that night if Joni had not turned on that light. I had made up my mind which way to go. I was ready to start swimming in the wrong direction when he turned on the light. That light in Joni's hand was my salvation that night.

Joni and I gathered up our gear, checked out the Suzuki, fired it up and headed up the trail to Pudak. We were greeted with great enthusiasm and excitement. Joni told our story in Bekua as I sipped a cup of hot *kopi susu*. Soon, I gathered my strength and my gear and went out behind the church building to change into dry clothes for the service.

I do not remember what I preached that night. I just know that I could have spoken in English instead of Indonesian, and those folks would have been just as happy with what I said. They were just excited that *pendeta kami* (our pastor) had come to celebrate Christmas with them.They listened to the message. They sang the songs of praise. They clapped their hands, praised God, and prayed and rejoiced and celebrated until the early hours of the morning. Sometime before dawn, Joni and I were shown to our rooms. I did not even bother to hang up my mosquito net. I just wrapped my sarong around me and fell into an exhausted sleep.

Sometime later the sun shining in my face and the smell of fresh coffee brought me out of my sleep. Joni and I had breakfast and led another worship service in which I shared the gospel message. We ate lunch, packed up our gear and made the four-hour trip back to Menjalin.

Carolyn was very glad to see me safely back. All sorts of rumors had reached Menjalin about my trip. All contained elements of truth—muddy roads, endless rain, cold and blackness, a flooded river, a fall from a bridge ("Again?" Carolyn thought. "What is it with Wayne and these bridges? One of these days one of these bridges kill him! Please, God, bring him home safe!") My arrival in Menjalin, of course, dispelled all the rumors of my untimely death.

A Light in My Understanding

It was only in the days following the trip to Pudak that I realized God had answered my question: Why am I here? Why did I have to leave my home, my family, and my people to serve in West Kalimantan, Indonesia? The answer came with great clarity as I read Isaiah 42:1–9. Isaiah wrote of God's promise to send a messenger via Israel who would become a shining light to the Gentiles, the non-Hebrew nations of the earth. The messenger would be a bright light shining in a dark place. His light would bring justice, peace, and freedom to the nations living in darkness. His light would show the nations where to go to find salvation!

Joni had been a bright light for me on the trail to Pudak. When he turned on that flashlight I knew where to go to find help and safety, to find salvation. Without that light, I would have died that night.

In the same way, God had sent me as "a prophet to the nations" in West Kalimantan. My job was to be a shining light in a very dark place. I was to shine the light of the gospel in a region held captive in the darkness of sin and the worship of a demon spirit named Jubata.

I was not the only one shining in that dark place, but God wanted me there. I was to preach the gospel.

Dayak Idols

78

I was to encourage my Dayak brothers and sisters to preach the gospel. I was to lead Dayaks to faith in Jesus, teach them to lead others to faith in Jesus, and ensure that the light of the gospel would flame brightly in the region for years to come.

The only way this could happen was if I, like Abraham, left my father's control and house. I had to get out of his sphere of influence so I could listen clearly to the leading of the Holy Spirit. If I remained in my father's house, he would control my work—not the Holy Spirit. If I remained in my own town, I would never learn to trust God for food, health, safety, or spiritual power. I could get all those things from my own city, and I would not learn to trust God alone to supply my needs. If I remained among my own people, many Dayaks would never hear the gospel. I would never be there to tell them about Jesus. My colleagues in ministry would be unable to carry out my work in my absence. Someone would never hear the gospel if I stayed in the United States.

In this way I came to understand the power of the call of God on the human soul. It is a call to true discipleship. It is a call to take up the cross of Christ, deny my own desires and the desires of my father. It was a call to follow Christ alone as the supreme ruler of my life. This is the greatest lesson a child of God and a minister of the gospel must learn. We must follow God wherever He leads us. For some, it will lead to missionary work in a foreign land. For some, it will lead into the business world or into academia. Wherever God leads, it requires total commitment to Him. This is true Christian discipleship.

So what motivates a person to leave their home, family, and culture? What motivates a person to learn a new language and culture? For me, it was the call of God on my life. It was the choice between taking up my cross to follow Jesus or staying at home in my own culture, under my father's authority, where I would have an easy life with all the comforts of home. It was a choice between my temporary comfort and many Dayaks spending eternity in hell.

Chapter 4

DO YOU EVER THINK ABOUT LEAVING?

During 1982–85 we lived in Jelimpo. Together with eight to ten national pastors and the PPIK[4] district leadership, I was responsible to oversee the ministry in twenty-two organized churches and twenty to thirty preaching points in District VIII of the PPIK. Every Sunday morning I visited one of the organized churches to preach, meet with the believers, encourage the pastor, and counsel those with specific issues. On Wednesday evenings, I visited preaching points for the same reasons. Often I would visit preaching points on Tuesday and Thursday evenings as well.

In addition to these duties, I was responsible to lead KAPJE (Congregational Leadership Bible Course), an elders training program. Elders from various PPIK districts were invited to Jelimpo for five nights and four days of Bible teaching. The intent was to equip them to lead their congregations more effectively by training them to share the gospel, teach basic Bible truths and stories, and to train their fellow elders how to study the Bible on their own.

Our House and PPIK District Office in Jelimpo

Dayak Village Church Leaders

I made all the arrangements for the KAPJE events. This included coordinating the dates with the national leadership of the districts and with my missionary colleagues, arranging for various leaders to present the

Bible teaching, and preparing to teach various subjects myself. Carolyn, along with the schoolgirls who lived with us, provided all the meals for twenty to fifty elders during the week. It was a very effective program.

Wayne Teaching in Jelimpo

During June, July, and August we would receive Project Timothy teams from the United States and Canada. Project Timothy (PT) was a program offered by my mission board to introduce American college students to life and ministry as missionaries. Our board hoped that exposure to missionary life would create a desire to devote their lives to serving God and humanity as missionaries around the world. Missionaries on furlough would be assigned to speak at Bible colleges and seminaries in hopes that God would move some students to consider missionary service. Interested students could apply to spend a summer working with experienced field personnel. As field staff we were asked to host PT summer workers.

Two specific events, both of which involved PT workers, speak powerfully to the importance of a strong sense of God's call to missionary service. Without it, very few remain long on mission for the King. My ministry with several summer workers provides a vivid example of this truth. These specific events were the ministry in Lumar and a PT worker's question.

The Lumar Ministry Plan

Sometime during my Jelimpo years, I hosted two groups of PT Summer Workers. As part of the experience of the first group, I planned a trip into the village of Lumar with the two male summer workers. My plan was to spend a full week in Lumar, conducting a vacation Bible school (VBS) for the children during the day and a Bible conference during the evening for the adults. Our goals were to increase biblical knowledge, motivate believers to greater discipleship, and inspire greater devotion to Jesus Christ. Serving Lumar, though, was a very complicated, very challenging matter.

Flag-Raising at Public School

84

Getting to Lumar was full of challenges, as there was no easy way to make the trip. The simplest way was to walk. It was an eight-hour trek from Anik, a small town where our mission had resident staff and operated a medical clinic. Another option was to go by river-boat. This was easier, but longer—two full days heading up river. The best way was to call MAF and arrange a flight to the Lumar airstrip, but even that was filled with challenges!

The first challenge was getting the flights scheduled. I could not call MAF like I was calling a taxi. Flight requests had to be submitted to MAF at least one full week before the day of the flight. MAF would arrange its schedule, giving priorities to flights as MAF deemed appropriate. They would do their best to meet our requests, but there were many variables—other flight requests, weather, and pilot availability and health; all would affect how our flights would be scheduled.

We had to contact the Lumar leaders to ensure the airstrip was ready. The airstrip was like the private airstrips operated by large farmers in the United States. It was unpaved and covered with grass (*lalang*). The grass could exceed a yard in height, and would have to be cut before the plane could land.

Cutting the grass on a Borneo airstrip was a major task. There were no machines to cut the grass nor any rakes to move it off the airstrip; it all had to be done by hand. I learned by personal experience that it required four days for five men working from early morning to early evening, with a two-hour break during the hottest part of the day, to cut the grass on an airstrip 550 yards long and 55 yards wide. The grass had to be cut by swinging a machete at ground level. Then long poles cut from the jungle were used to push the meter-long grass to the side of the airstrip so the plane could land. It was a major undertaking, and one that would require the participation of all in the village for it to be completed in time for our arrival.

MAF had strict regulations about the condition of landing strips. Tall grass could bunch up under the plane's wheels, causing it to flip over. Tall grass could also conceal objects, like tree limbs or termite mounds, which would cause the plane to flip over.

Before landing, the pilot would circle the strip to check it out. If it appeared safe, he would land. If he saw anything that concerned him, he would refuse to land and take us back to Jelimpo. Even if the pilot refused to land, I still had to pay for the flight! I needed to inform the Lumar church leaders at least a week in advance, so they could cut the grass and clear the strip.

MAF subsidized the costs of the flights, but it was still an expensive way to travel. One flight could easily consume my salary for the entire month. I did not have the money to pay for this. The PT workers brought some funds for ministry, but they did not have enough to pay for these flights, either. The summer workers were big men, and we would have a lot of baggage since we would be taking materials for the VBS—crafts for the kids, study guides, song books, and Bibles—all the things we would need for a week of ministry. We would need at least two shuttles from Jelimpo. It was an expensive trip.

Where was I to get funding for the flights? One of my assigned duties on the field was to the Christian Education Committee (CEC). This was a mission committee formed to promote Christian education throughout the regions served by our organization and its national church. As a member of the committee I knew that it had funds for Christian education ministries, and the committee eagerly promoted VBS programs. I thought this was a great opportunity to use some of these funds.

My ministry plan would provide a VBS program in Lumar. As I considered it, I realized that I could also arrange for VBS programs to be conducted in two additional villages, Sengkeru and Sekamu. These two villages could be reached by boat from Lumar without difficulty. Sengkeru was only an hour down river from Lumar, and Sekamu another hour beyond Sengkeru. If I took four *Dayak guru Injil* with me, a two-man team could conduct ministries in both these villages while the PT workers and I conducted the VBS in Lumar itself. The CEC should be willing to assist with the cost of the flights since three villages would be served, and I would share the costs with the PT workers and the CEC account. I thought it was a great idea, so I tried to contact the CEC committee chairperson to gain agreement and permission for the use of the funds.

The chairperson, however, was unavailable. She was traveling off the island. Cell phones were unimagined in the 1980s, so there was no way I could contact her to ask for authorization to use CEC funds for this ministry. What was I to do?

I contacted my field director. This man was responsible to oversee all of our mission operations in West Kalimantan. He was always invited to the CEC meetings, so he was familiar with its goals, policies, and resources. He was also authorized to make decisions regarding field ministries when necessary. So I took this matter to him. I explained the purposes of the Lumar ministry trip. I presented the plan, the goals, the potential benefits, the travel complications, the funding needs, and the unavailability of the CEC chairperson. I asked him to authorize the use of the CEC funds for this ministry. After extensive discussion and review of all the details, he authorized the use of the funds.

With funds secured, I made the arrangements. I sent letters with messengers to the church elders in Lumar. I gave them the plans and the dates. I asked them to inform the believers in Sengkeru and Sekamu. I scheduled the flights with MAF. I recruited four Dayak brothers to conduct VBS programs in Sengkeru and Sekamu. I contacted other CEC members to secure the VBS materials and arranged to transport them to Jelimpo. I trained the PT workers to help with the VBS. They would help with the crafts and games; I would do the teaching. I would translate their devotionals and testimonies in the evening Bible conference. I reviewed the VBS materials with the Dayak men, helped them plan a series of messages for their evening Bible conferences, and helped them work out a schedule to share the work in the villages. Carolyn prepared medical kits for the Dayaks to take with them to the village, and trained them on which pills to use for various ailments that regularly troubled us on these village ministry trips. On the night before the flights to Lumar, we gathered at Jelimpo for prayer and planning. Everything was ready.

The Flights to Lumar

The MAF plane arrived on schedule. The weather was good—clear skies, low winds. I took time to chat with the pilot to explain our plans and all the work invested in this trip. I explained how extensive our ministry would be from these two flights. He prayed with me before he began loading the plane.

The two PT workers and I took the first flight. I wanted to be with the pilot when he made his decision about landing on the Lumar airstrip. If there were problems, I wanted to be on site so I could make wise decisions. The second flight would transport the four Dayaks, the VBS materials, and the remainder of the baggage.

It is only a short distance from Jelimpo to Lumar as a bird flies. As the airstrip came into view, the pilot pointed it out to me. It was a tiny strip of green grass in the middle of a vast virgin jungle. As we approached I could see women and children running on the airstrip. It was normal for the kids to do this. They were always excited about a plane landing on the strip, but it was unusual to see the women dashing down the strip. I wondered if my messages about our plans had reached the village. If the news had not reached them, this would be very interesting.

Dayak Village Airstrip

As the pilot circled the field to check out the condition of the airstrip, he said nothing. I prayed. When the pilot circled a second time, I began to worry. Something was wrong. I looked closer at the strip. The grass had not been cut. Normally, grass higher than the wheels would cause the pilot to cancel the flight. After the second pass, and without saying a word to me, the pilot put the plane into a steep turn, lined up with the airstrip, and set the plane down safely. Those pilots were amazing!

As the PT workers unloaded our gear, and the villagers swarmed around the plane, the pilot and I examined the airstrip. The grass was knee high, but sparse enough that the pilot thought it safe to land. He explained that he would make the shuttle to get us all into Lumar, but that he would not land at the end of the week to fly us out unless the grass was cut and cleared off the strip. I assured him I would discuss this with the local leaders and have news for him when he returned with the Dayak men and our baggage. The pilot then departed for Jelimpo.

I immediately found the church elder. With evident excitement he explained that word had reached them that we were coming, and that all was ready in Lumar, Sengkeru, and Sekamu. Everyone was excited and eager to hear the Word of God. His excitement was dampened when I asked about the grass on the strip.

No one wanted to cut the grass. All were busy in their rice fields, and they just could not take time now to cut it. I explained that it had to be cut before we could leave. He said there was nothing he could do. Folks just did not want to work on the strip at this time. If they took time out of the fields to cut the grass, they would not want to attend the Bible conference. It was impossible to get it cut during the week.

It was a simple matter. If the grass was not cut, the pilot would not return in a week to fly us out. The grass could not be cut in time. So, we either had to cancel the ministry and fly out immediately or find another way out of Lumar. I whispered a quick prayer. "Lord, what do I do now?" Then I began to walk the airstrip to check its condition.

What I found was frightening! Halfway down the strip, village women had stacked up firewood. They had cut the wood in the jungle beside the airstrip and stacked it on the strip until they had opportunity to carry it to their homes. There were several stacks, each knee high. As I stood there looking at the stacks of wood I could see the tracks of the plane when it landed. It was less than a yard from the stack of wood. If the plane had passed one yard to the side it would have hit the firewood, flipped over, burst into flame, and incinerated all on board. I immediately began throwing the wood off the strip into the jungle. The church elder saw what I was doing and called for the villagers to help. Frantically we worked to get that wood off the strip before the plane returned.

I did not tell the pilot about the wood. I just told him to cancel the flights scheduled to take us out. We would find another way home. I was not willing to put his life at risk by asking him to make another flight when I knew the villagers would not be willing to cut the grass. He replied, "I think that is a wise decision."

My Dayak hosts were chagrined by the poor condition of the airstrip, and completely agreed with my decision to cancel the flights out. My Dayak ministry team agreed as well. They were at home in the jungle and in Dayak villages, so it was not a problem for them. My PT colleagues were not as sanguine about it. They were filled with questions. How do we get out? What do we do? I explained that I had no idea. I would have to work it out with our hosts.

Soon, the Dayak team members and their gear were loaded on a motorboat. I gathered the PT workers and the church elders to pray for them as they departed. We watched them until the boat disappeared around the bend of the river. Then we turned to the task at hand, preaching the gospel in Lumar.

The Work in Lumar

We began the Bible conference that night. All the villagers turned out. There was singing and Bible readings. Young people formed groups and sang special numbers; the men sang, and the women sang. The PT workers each told the story of how he came to know Jesus personally. I preached the gospel. The people were blessed and edified. God was glorified. All were encouraged. These meetings were held every night, Monday through Friday. Every night more people came. People from distant villages heard about the special meetings and came to see what the Americans would do. They wanted to hear the funny things we would say as we tried to use their language. It was good entertainment in this remote Borneo jungle. As word spread, more came. No service was conducted on Saturday night so all could prepare for Sunday.

Every morning we conducted the VBS. The leaders of the Lumar youth group led the singing. The children loved to sing, and the youth leaders knew their favorite songs. The PT workers learned the songs, and even sang special numbers to show how well they had mastered the Indonesian songs. The children laughed endlessly at their mistakes and began to mimic their American pronunciation of Indonesian.

Both groups of helpers, the Dayak young people and the PT workers, helped the children with crafts from the VBS materials. They colored the simple drawings that illustrated the Bible story and took them home to show their parents. Every child was excited to explain the meaning of the picture to his or her parents. This greatly encouraged the parents to come to the evening meetings. They wanted to color pictures, too!

Every morning I taught a Bible story. The materials we used were prepared for American children, so I had to adapt the stories and the applications to fit the Dayak world and culture. Every story was biblically based. It presented the gospel in a clear way, simple enough that all could understand. For five days, Tuesday through Saturday (we arrived too late to conduct the VBS on Monday morning), the children came to sing, draw, color, play games, and hear about Jesus and His love for them.

Sunday morning had the largest attendance of the week. Hundreds came. People from every village in the region came. The church was filled. The benches were dangerously full! A dozen people crowded into a space normally used by eight, and little children sat on the laps of those lucky enough to get a space on the bench.

When the crowd continued to push into the church grass mats were placed on the floor in front of the altar for the children to use. Adults flooded in to fill the benches. The windows were filled with those who

93

could not get into the church. Happy faces gazed in to see the show!

The show was a great one! Every church in the district had a special song to sing. The youth groups from many churches had to sing. Local military, government, and political leaders were present, and all were invited to say a few words of greeting. It was a big event, and everyone wanted to participate.

The PT workers were next. They thanked the Lumar leaders for their hospitality and warm friendship, and gave their testimonies. They explained how God revealed Himself to them, how he changed their lives, and how important he was in their daily lives in America. They challenged all present to turn from evil and put their trust fully in Jesus Christ.

I preached. I told the story of Jesus and his love. It was the old, old story starting from the days of angels in Bethlehem. It was the story told to the tribes of Germany by Roman monks. It was the same story told by the Irish monks to the Viking invaders. It was the same story told by William Carey in India and James Hudson Taylor in China. I declared his glory — creation, sin, judgment, incarnation, crucifixion, resurrection, ascension, and proclamation to all tribes on earth. I preached the gospel!

People responded. Lives were changed. Eternal destinies were altered. The angels rejoiced that new names were now recorded in the Lamb's Book of Life. It was a powerful week of ministry.

It was hard work, but it was worth it. Now, it was time to go home.

The Way Out of Lumar

After the flights were canceled, we had to find another way out of Lumar. There were many options, but most were impractical.

We could walk, but we had too much baggage for us to carry it all. Each us had our own clothes and personal needs for a week in the remote village. We had our Bible and songbooks. We had some extra Bibles and songbooks we took along to sell to folks who were unable to travel out to the market towns where they could purchase their own books. We had unused craft materials, drawings to color, crayons and markers—all the things we needed for the VBS. We needed to take the unused items with us so they could be used in other villages. We could not carry our personal items and the additional materials. If we walked out, we would have to hire local folks to carry the extra baggage for us. We would also have to pay for their meals and provide a place for them to stay in the market town until their return to Lumar. It would be expensive to hire them, and it would mean at least eight hours walking through the jungle to Anik. Then we would need to spend the night at a mission station there, and take public transport home the following day. We could do it, but it was not something any of us was eager to do.

The Plan

We could go by boat. Another mission organization had donated to the Lumar church a large boat suitable for use on the rivers of West Kalimantan. We decided to lease the boat and crew to take us downriver to Ngabang, the market town near to Jelimpo. The boat was large enough to handle my seven-man team, our baggage, and the crew. We would have enough room to sit comfortably in the boat and relax on the trip. We could talk over the events of the week. We could consider how to improve the VBS program, how to continue the ministry in the area, and how to provide consistent ministry in the region. We could pray. We could rest!

Village Riverboat as Used in Lumar

I contacted the crew and made the arrangements. We would leave early on Monday morning. The crew would have the boat ready for a dawn departure. The PT workers and I would carry our gear down to the boat in the morning darkness. We would load up and head downriver.

An hour downriver we would stop at Sengkeru to pick up the first team. I would have to spend some time visiting with the local Christian leaders and the important people of the village. I welcomed the opportunity to meet the elders. Denominational and mission leaders rarely visited this church. Most would stop at Lumar and expect these leaders to make the long trip upriver to meet them there. Seldom, indeed, would a missionary or an ordained national pastor visit the village. So I knew the stop would take at least an hour, possibly even two hours.

Then we would continue downriver to Sekamu to pick up the second team. Here, again, I would have to visit with the local leaders. It was possible to reach Sekamu by road from Anik, so denominational leaders visited here more often than to Lumar or Sengkeru, but it was a rarity for missionaries to visit. It was an even stranger thing for two young Americans to visit. It was a great plan. However, plans are often far different from reality.

Delayed Departure

We had to wait for breakfast before we could depart. The village leaders had instructed our host family to wait for them to join us for breakfast. No one told us about this. We were packed and ready to go before the first glimmer of dawn appeared in the sky. Our hosts insisted we could not leave until we had our coffee and breakfast. So we waited. We stacked our gear on the veranda of the house, sat on the grass mats in the front room of the house, and waited—for an hour!

As the sun lightened the eastern sky, the village leaders appeared. Breakfast was served. We had a great meal and great fellowship. When I rose to leave, the elders told me to wait. The elders wanted to give us a formal send-off. Each had special words of thanks, testimonies of God's blessing though our ministry, and invitations for us to visit again. They closed with a prayer of blessing; then we were free to go. It was now after seven o'clock in the morning—an hour later than my planned departure time. We gathered our gear and headed to the river, where another change of plans was forced on us.

As we approached the landing where the boat was tied, we saw a huge crowd of people waiting. I assumed they came to see us off, to wish us safe journey. As we neared the boat, and it became obvious we were ready to board and depart, the entire crowd of people jumped or climbed onto the boat! My team and I stood there in total confusion. The boat was already full. There was no room for us and no room for our baggage. Even more, there was no room for the four team members we had to pick up in Sengkeru and Sekamu.

I knew immediately what was happening. I had charted the boat to make the trip to Ngabang. All expenses were mine. Everyone else wanted a free ride to town and back. No one asked if they could go with us. They just assumed they could go and hopped on the boat. They scrambled on board as soon as they saw us because they knew there was insufficient room for all who wanted to go. Each claimed a spot on the boat, and the last one in would be left behind. The problem was I and my two colleagues were the last ones.

I turned back up the path to the village. I told the PT workers to follow me. We would walk to Anik. In full confusion, they followed me. The folks on the boat began to call to me. I continued walking up the path back to the village. Finally, the boat captain came running up to me, asking where I was going. I told him I was going to find a guide and some helpers so we could walk to Anik. He was not happy.

The discussions lasted for half an hour. I told the captain that since the boat was already full we would just have to find another way to Anik. He replied there was plenty of room for us. We debated the issue at length, but the crux of the problem was a cultural difference of how much room a person needed. I wanted a flat seat with a backrest, a place to stretch out my legs, room to move about as the hours passed. I wanted room for each of my team members, too. I also wanted the baggage to be stowed away so we did not have to hold it. The Dayaks thought that a spot on the gunwales was sufficient on which to sit and our baggage could be under our feet or on our laps—for the ten to twelve hours it would take to reach Ngabang.

There were also different expectations about who was paying for this trip. I explained that since I was paying for the entire boat, I wanted the use of the entire boat. This would give my team and I time to talk about the ministry as I had planned. The captain insisted that the others would not interfere with our travel; since I was paying for the trip anyway, there was no reason the others should have to pay anything. Our comfort and plans for work on the trip were not a consideration. This was the way they always did things. After extensive discussion, we negotiated an agreement.

The terms were very specifically stated. The captain would return to the boat and clear space for the team and our baggage. He and the village folks, not us, would decide who would be left behind. All those who made the trip with us would pay the normal fare for a trip to Ngabang. I would pay the normal fare for my team and my baggage. Payment would be made at Ngabang. With this understanding, the captain returned to the boat. When all was ready, he called us to get on board.

Our baggage had been stowed in the center of the boat, under all the baggage of the village travelers. A small space was reserved for me on the last seat at the rear of the boat. The PT workers each had a space on the gunwale, one on each side of the boat so that their weight would balance out and reduce chances for capsizing. Four Lumar people would stop at Sekamu so there would be room for my four colleagues serving in the villages downriver. We finally left the landing at eight o'clock.

The Language Problem

It was August, the dry season in West Kalimantan. The water level of the river was low. Our captain had explained it would be a challenge to make the trip to Ngabang because the low water level made deadfalls and sandbars a major concern. I thought he was just using it as a bargaining strategy. He could claim it was more expensive to travel now because he would need an extra boat hand and more fuel to maneuver around the obstacles. When the water was high, he could float over these things; but with low water he had to seek out clear paths or portage around barriers. Less than an hour from Lumar, I learned he was not just negotiating a higher fare.

We were making good time in clear, deep water as we came around a bend in the river. The crew member in the bow shouted a warning, but it was too late. We ran up on a tree that had fallen in the river. Our speed and the force of the current pushed the boat up onto the trunk of the tree. We came to a sudden, jarring stop as the boat keel slammed onto the trunk. All but the captain and crew were thrown off their feet or slid down into the bottom of the boat, but no damage was done. The PT workers and I were sitting in the bow, right behind the crewman so we could see what was happening.

The captain shouted orders, and the crew immediately jumped into the water to free the boat. They knew that as the crew left the boat, it would rise in the water (due to the lighter load). The boat could be pushed over the trunk, and we could continue the trip. It was a common experience for travel on the Behe River. No big deal.

One of the PT workers was a tall, lean, muscular guy. He was always eager to help and to try new things. He saw the boat crew at work, understood they needed to lighten the boat, and wanted to help. He stood up, turned to me and asked,

"Should I get out and help?"

One thing I had learned about traveling in a boat with Dayaks was that they did not need my help. Whatever the challenge or problem, the best and most helpful thing I could do was sit down, stay out of the way, and let these experienced boatmen do their job. The last thing they needed was for a clumsy American stumbling about trying to help! He would only make things worse. So I knew the best thing for the PT workers and I to do was to sit down and stay out of the way.

"*Jangan*" I told the guy.

He looked at me for a moment, and then he asked again, "Should I get out and help?"

"*Jangan*" I said, raising my voice to ensure he could hear me over the noise of the engine and the shouting of the crew.

By now crew members were standing on the trunk of the tree with water up to their knees. All were shoving the boat forward, but we were still too heavy. The boat was making very slow progress. Seeing them struggling with the boat, the worker again turned to me and shouted, "Should I get out and help?"

Emphatically I shouted, "*Jangan*."

Then I watched in amazement as the silly young man placed one hand on the gunwale and vaulted into the river. He disappeared under the water like a stone! Only the tips of his fingers held onto the gunwale. I lunged forward just in time to grab his wrist as his fingers were pulled from the gunwale by the force of the current. If I had missed his wrist, he would have been washed under the boat into the branches of the fallen tree. Only God knows if or where he would have emerged. To this day I am convinced that if he had been washed under, he would have been trapped by branches snagging his clothes and drowned.

The other PT worker quickly joined me, as did a couple of the villagers who saw what was happening. Together we pulled the guy back into the boat. Moments later the boat was freed from the tree, and we were again moving smoothly downstream. As the guy sat up in the boat, I began to berate him.

"Why did you do that?" I shouted. "I told you three times not to do it!"

"All you said was '*Jangan*'" he replied.

"Yes!" I replied. "Three times! Why did you still do it?" I shouted again.

"Well, what does '*Jangan*' mean?" He shouted back at me. Suddenly I understood! I answered him in Indonesian! He did not understand Indonesian! No wonder he asked three times! I did not realize I was speaking Indonesian to him. I was so used to speaking the language, I did not realize I was not using English.

I apologized profusely. Then all three of us started laughing! We just laughed! Then the Dayaks began laughing, too. They were all hiding their laughter, not wanting to embarrass us, but once we started laughing, they could no longer hide their mirth.

As the laughter died away, the PT worker who was now shivering from the cool breeze whipping over his soaked clothing, asked a question.

"Wayne, why did I go so deep in the water while Dayaks were only in water up to their knees? I am way taller than they are, so how come I went so deep into the water?"

"They were standing on the tree trunk! You just went into the river!" I explained.

Then we just started laughing again!

The Village of Sengkeru

Our arrival at Sengkeru was expected, so I was surprised when no one was waiting at the landing when we arrived. Curious, I stepped ashore and followed the path up to the village. As always, the children were the first to see the foreigner. They came running up, yelling and laughing and talking excitedly to one another in their local dialect. All were eager to see what I would do, to touch my skin, pull the hair on my arms—it was always the same routine when I entered a new village. Of course, some of the smaller ones were afraid; but as long as I kept smiling and did not get too close, they would hold onto their older siblings' arm or leg and watch with big eyes the strange doings of this strange man with white skin and hair on his face.

"Di mana Pak Anwardi?" I asked, hoping that at least one of them would understand my Indonesian. One boy with a big gap-toothed grin replied instantly. Pointing the way to a large house in the center of the village he said, *"Di situ, Pak! Di rumah kepala kampung!"* Wonderful, I thought. Anwardi is paying his respects to the village headman. We should be able to leave soon if all the amenities and formalities have been completed.

As I mounted the notched log that served as steps up to the veranda, the children swarmed around, noisily announcing my arrival. The headman's wife greeted me, which was a bit unusual; normally the headman himself came to welcome visitors at the door. It was his responsibility to evaluate all visitors and determine if they were to be welcomed to the village. I assumed he knew who was coming, since the children had announced my arrival, so he felt it appropriate to send his wife to the door.

As I was ushered into the front room of the house, I found Anwardi sitting with the headman in serious discussion. They were seated in the only two chairs in the room, with a small table between them. Empty teacups, and an empty teapot indicated they had been there for a while. They paused in their conversation long enough to offer a word of welcome and invite me to have a seat on the grass mats spread on the floor. Again, I was a bit surprised. Normally, headmen would offer me the chair, asking Anwardi to sit on the floor. This breach of standard protocol was unusual, so I watched carefully to see what would happen next.

Village Tea Service

The headman turned to Anwardi and said, *"Kalau begitu, Pak Guru, bagaimanakah kami berladang? Tanpa korban hasil ladang kami kosong."*

Ah! Now I understood! The village headman wanted to know how to make a successful rice crop if he turned to Christ and no longer followed the old ways. They spoke in dialect—either Banana or Bakua. I could not distinguish between the two and could only understand bits and pieces of either, but I was able to follow the main points as the discussion continued.

The headman wanted to know how Christians should make their rice fields. The old ways called for a series of seven sacrifices throughout the rice cycle. If these were not appropriately done, Jubata, the spirit controlling the rice harvest, would withhold his blessing and the harvest would be poor. The headman wanted to know if Jesus would help them with their "daily bread." Would Jesus enable them to grow rice? If not, they would starve, so it would be better to continue to follow the old ways.

Dayak Offering in Rice Field

Anwardi quietly and patiently explained the power of Jesus Christ as The Word, the one by whom the Father, the Great High God, created the universe. He explained how The Word was one with the Father, as a human son is one with his own father. He assured the headman that as creator of the universe, Jesus had greater power than Jubata and was able to grant a great harvest, better than Jubata could give.

Hearing this I nervously shifted position on the grass mat. I feared that Anwardi was falling into the mistake of the "prosperity gospel" preachers who often toured though West Kalimantan. They promised God would make the believer rich if only they had enough faith, and demonstrated that faith by giving a good offering to the preacher. I did not want these villagers to learn to think in that way.

I need not have worried though. Anwardi addressed the issue quickly. He explained that Jesus could give great harvests, but there was no guarantee of wealth and riches. Jesus promised that He would always provide the "daily bread" his people needed. He explained that as we seek God first and obey His will, His blessing will be on us. Whether we prosper or not, if we are faithful to Him, we will be blessed. We will always have enough.

"So what do I do instead of the sacrifices?" the headman asked.

Anwardi suggested the head of the family lead in prayer at each of the times when a sacrifice would normally be offered. He suggested that families working adjacent fields could gather together to pray before starting work. They could pray daily, or they could pray at the normal sacrifice times. They could pray at home or in the field. They could sing a hymn or a chorus. All of these things would be pleasing to the Creator.

Anwardi and Bride on Their Wedding Day

For more than hour I sat quietly, sipping coffee as I listened to Anwardi explain how a Christian Dayak should live in the jungles of West Kalimantan. I did not understand it all—they were using the local dialect—but I understood enough to know that God had done a great work through Anwardi and his colleague during this week of ministry. This village, and its neighboring villages, had heard the gospel explained powerfully for a full week, and many had been transferred from the kingdom of darkness to the Kingdom of Light! The gospel was moving across the natural bridges of family ties to reach into other distant villages. The entire region was affected by one week of VBS and Bible preaching. Praise God Almighty, I thought. It was worth it! All the trouble and work and money invested was not wasted! Lives were changed and eternal destinies altered!

Finally we returned to the boat, prayed for our brothers and sisters in Christ, said farewell, and departed for Sekamu.

The Village of Sekamu

When we arrived in Sekamu, I walked up to the village to find my team. I found them at the church. A closing service had just ended, and the crowd was now heading down to the river to talk with friends from Lumar. Others followed me back to the church, and then to the headman's house.

The headman served us coffee and sticky rice as he shared his excitement about what God had done in the village. He told stories of reconciled relationships, repentant thieves, and reformed drunkards, and many other changes brought about by God through the preaching of the team members. He was also very appreciative of the VBS program. The children were excited about the crafts they had made. The mothers were delighted that someone cared about their children. The fathers were pleased that the children were learning new things, and their horizons for the future were enlarged. The headman had only one request for me.

"Please," he said, "Do this again soon! We need this for the growth and development of our people."

"I will do all that I can, but only God knows the future." I replied.

Again, I thought, it was worth every penny spent. It was worth all the work and planning and travel. God had blessed these people. His name was glorified and his message, the gospel, preached. Blessed be the name of the Lord! My mind was filled with joy as we departed Sekamu.

The Rest of the Journey

The rest of the journey was uneventful. We pressed on as fast as possible, hoping to arrive in Ngabang in time to get a local public transport vehicle back to Jelimpo. We still had to portage around rocky rapids at two places, though. It took time for all the people to disembark at the portage site, walk around the rapids, and then embark again. We pressed on with all possible speed, but the sun was dropping faster than we could travel. It was well after dark when we arrived at Ngabang.

Deception and Betrayal

As we disembarked at Ngabang, I was surprised to see the villagers who traveled with us remain seated on the boat. The crew gathered our baggage and started up the path to the bus station, where we hoped to secure transport to Jelimpo. I turned to the captain and asked how much I owed him for the fare for my team. He replied we would settle up at the coffee shop by the bus station.

This troubled me. I feared that once we left the boat, the others would scatter without paying their fares, and the captain would be left to cover expenses on his own. I did not want this to happen. The captain deserved to be paid, and I wanted to pay my share now, so he could then collect from the others. The captain refused my offer to settle up and again urged us to continue to the bus station. He was worried we would be too late to get transport and have problems about where to spend the night in Ngabang. Reluctantly, I joined my team as they headed up to the bus station.

In the coffee shop I arranged for my team and the captain and his crew to have a good rice meal. All were very tired and hungry after the long journey. Rice with curried chicken, spiced beef, fried potatoes, pork in soy sauce, and cassava leaves—all these delicious Indonesian dishes were served and more beside! We all ate hearty meals and washed it down with delicious ice-cold tea with lime! Refreshed by food and drink, content with a great ministry, and eager to reach home, I again asked the captain what I owed him for our passage.

In typical Dayak fashion, the captain did not state the price. Instead he began to remind me of all our discussions back in Lumar. He explained how difficult the trip was, and that now he had to make the return journey. He had to find accommodations in Ngabang and feed his crew until they left for Lumar. I interrupted his discourse and asked bluntly, in typical American fashion,

"How much, sir?"

He finally stated an amount. It was the full amount for the charter of the boat from Lumar to Ngabang, with additional payment for room and board for the crew to stay two nights in Ngabang. He expected me to pay the total costs. The villagers who joined us on the trip were to ride free, at my expense.

Stifling my anger and speaking very quietly and softly I reminded the captain of our agreement in Lumar. I was to pay only the costs for my team. The villagers were to pay their normal fares. I was not prepared to change the agreement. I would not pay more than we had agreed.

The captain replied that the people were poor and had no money. They had already left the boat and scattered. So even if some had money, it was now impossible for him to collect from them. We debated the matter for another thirty minutes, until Anwardi informed me he had secured a ride for us back to Jelimpo. Public transport was no longer available—all had made their last runs for the night—but Anwardi had met a friend who was riding in the back of a delivery truck on the way to Sanggau. The driver had agreed to let us ride in the back of the truck to Jelimpo for free, but we had to leave now.

There really was nothing I could do about the boat fare. If I refused to pay, my reputation in the entire Lumar area would be ruined. The captain would return there and report that I had refused to pay the fare, that I cheated him, that Christians could not be trusted to pay their bills, and more beside. I would have no way to counteract these lies. Future visits to the area would be difficult. The new believers in the region would be embarrassed by my actions. The reputation of Christ and the Church would suffer. So I decided to suffer loss rather than bring disrepute on the Name. I paid the captain all that he required. I even added a bit extra to show that I appreciated his hard work on my behalf. I hated being cheated, deceived, and betrayed. I was angry that they had lied to me, and I had no recourse. But for the sake of the Name, I kept silent and led the team back to Jelimpo. It was great to be home again!

The Question

Shortly after our return, the PT workers moved on to visit other mission ministries, and a team of two young ladies, also PT workers, came to Jelimpo. These ladies worked closely with Carolyn for the week they stayed in Jelimpo. They helped with the children's meetings on Sunday morning by distributing craft materials and ink drawings depicting the Bible story she told, as well as the crayons to color the ink drawings.

Carolyn had them help with the ladies meetings held in our home after the Sunday morning worship service. They shared their personal testimonies, emphasizing how God had worked in their lives to call them into missionary service. They blessed the ladies with songs and words of encouragement. The ladies responded joyfully to them, asking questions about life in the United States, their goals in life, marriage prospects, and all the things that interest mothers around the world.

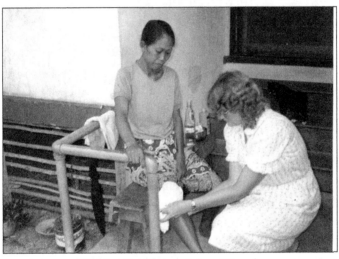

Carolyn Treating an Injured Dayak

The Dayak pastor of the local church invited them to speak to the church youth group. The Dayak girls wanted to know about life in the United States—about high school and college, about American boys, differences in dating practices, and if the girls were engaged. The boys were infatuated with their beautiful pale skin, now darkening under the tropical sun, and their ease in talking with them. Most Dayak girls at the time were not permitted to talk to boys, so it was an exciting thing to meet beautiful girls and actually talk to them!

Dayak Youth Group

In all these interactions, the PT ladies kept the focus on spiritual matters. They challenged the girls to live for Christ, to follow His leading in selecting a life partner, in deciding to pursue further education or marry and follow the traditional life in the village. They encouraged the boys to pursue further education to prepare themselves for the new world that was now emerging in their villages. They encouraged them to prepare for life in a modern society, knowing that the traditional village lifestyle would soon be a thing of the past.

I took them, along with Carolyn and our children, to midweek prayer meetings in nearby villages. We would walk the jungle trails to Kiru, Kayu Ara, and other villages where folks were eager to hear about Jesus. On the way they would banter with the Dayak youth who accompanied us, trying their best to communicate with the few Indonesian phrases and words they had mastered. They would teach the Dayaks American Christian songs, and the Dayak teens would teach them the same songs in Indonesian. In all these things, the PT ladies would demonstrate to the Dayaks that life in Christ was a joyful thing. Their winsome personalities drew the youth to Christ.

Crossing a Jungle Bridge

In the prayer meetings, I asked the ladies to sing Christian songs, give their testimony, or share a devotional thought or word of encouragement. The villagers were enthralled by these presentations. They were just amazed that these wonderful young people would travel halfway around the world just to meet them, to share their lives with them, and to drink tea and eat fried cassava dipped in *gula tebu* (syrup made from fresh-squeezed sugar cane) while sitting on grass mats on their floor in remote jungle homes.

One day as we were eating our midday meal at home in Jelimpo, one of the PT girls asked me a serious question.

"Wayne," she asked, "do you ever think about going home?"

"Every day!" I replied instantly without a moment's hesitation. "Every day! Every day I think about leaving and going home."

"Why?" she asked.

"Good question." I replied. I do not recall the exact words, but I know this is the essence of my response.

It is very difficult to be so far from home. My children do not know their grandparents. Our parents have not seen their grandchildren in four years. We write letters, and send photographs, but it is not the same. My parents long to be with my children. My mother wants to teach my daughter to sew and to cook. My father wants to teach my son to repair a car engine, to use a hammer and a saw, to put a new roof on a house, and to trim the trees in the yard. None of this is possible because we are here, and every day I think about going home, so my children may know their grandparents.

This separation became even more bitter when we learned my mother-in-law had cancer. We did not know how serious her condition was. Mothers do not want to frighten their children, and fathers rarely write the details of painful experiences in letters. All we could do was pray and hope for good news of improved health in the next letter from home.

Allen Family in Dayak Rice Field

Carolyn's father wrote of traveling to distant cities for new and improved treatments. Yet, there was never any word of improvement in her condition. After two months with no news, no letters, no word of any kind from home, we made the five-hour trip to Pontianak. We knew we could go to the phone company office and call home. (This was before cell phones, of course.) We wanted news because the whole situation was weighing heavily on Carolyn. She knew her mother was fighting for her life, and she longed to be there to help her mother in this desperate fight. Yes, we thought every day about going home.

In Pontianak we drove directly to the phone company office. I let Carolyn out of our Toyota Land Cruiser at the office door and told her to make the arrangements for the call. I would park the car and bring the kids to find her in the lobby. Carolyn hurried into the office, eager to speak with her mother again.

117

When the kids and I entered the office lobby I looked around for Carolyn. She was not in the waiting area, so I began looking in the phone booths where folks could make long-distance calls. She was not to be seen. Confused, I looked again at the long row of phone booths. There was a light over each booth to indicate it was in use. Every light was illuminated, showing every booth was in use. Then I noticed one booth was empty. In all the other booths the caller was visible through the glass window, but no one was visible in this one. I walked over to the booth and looked inside.

Carolyn was squatting down in the corner, in typical village fashion, with tears rushing down her face as she spoke with her father. Mother was gone. Father had just returned home from the funeral and for the first time sat down alone in the house where he and Mother had raised Carolyn.

Gently I raised Carolyn to her feet and took the phone. As Carolyn continued to cry on my shoulder and the children clung to me, I learned that Mother had died at home the previous week. Her strength failed, and she passed quietly into the presence of Jesus as her sisters and husband stood beside her. Carolyn's sister was there, too, as Mother departed. Carolyn was not there. Letters had been sent, but mail had been delayed. So this was the first we knew that Mother was gone. Yes, every day I thought about going home.

A year after Carolyn's mother passed into eternity, I received a message via the short-wave radio. A telegram for me had been delivered to the mission office that day. What did I want them to do? It had to be important for a telegram to be sent. I knew my mother was not well and thought the telegram would be about her. After a moment's thought I instructed them to put the letter in the mission guesthouse, where we stayed when we visited Pontianak.

It took me an hour to pack and prepare my Suzuki motorcycle, but I was on the road as soon as possible. Five hours later I reached the guesthouse. The telegram informed me that my mother was now in the hospital. Her lingering illness had worsened so that my father and my brother could not care for her at home. Her prognosis was not encouraging. Yes, I thought about going home. My family needed me, and I needed them. But in the morning I drove that Suzuki back to Jelimpo. I had to preach that weekend, but I thought about going home.

A week later I again received word via the short-wave radio that another telegram for me had been delivered to the office. I asked my colleague to read it to me. After a pause, she said, "It's not good news." Then I knew my mother had gone home to heaven. I wanted to go home, too. I longed to be there with my father and brother. They had no family in the city where I was raised. Mom and Dad had moved far from home to find work, so our family was only the four of us. My parents' families were far away. They needed me! I wanted to be there! Yes, I thought about going home.

I told the PT girls about these events, and how Carolyn and I longed to go home for the funerals; but we did not have the money for the flights. It was impossible to go.

Then I told the PT girls about the Lumar trip. I told them about the days of planning, the week in the village, the long boat ride back to Ngabang. I told them about being deceived about the costs of the boat. I told them that I thought about quitting and going home.

Then I told them about other events I had experienced. I told them about the day dozens of church leaders were traveling to Jelimpo for an elders' conference when their vehicle had a tire blow out while doing 55 mph. The vehicle flipped over on the road, scattering my people like matchsticks on the pavement. I told them about preaching to my elders, my brothers and sisters in Christ, that night. One of our own was dead. One was paralyzed, never to walk or use his hands or control his bladder again. Others were seriously injured and scarred for life. I preached on the hope and certainty of the resurrection that night. I preached, and I thought about going home.

Road Conditions

I told her about falling off a bridge on my motorcycle, of long motorcycle rides in near-hurricane force winds and rain, of long treks to distant villages, and longer nights sleeping on grass mats on uneven wooden floors. I told her of eating boiled frogs and wildcat meat. I told her of nearly dying of typhoid fever, of struggling with food poisoning, of innumerable bouts of vomiting and diarrhea, and even more mosquito bites. I told her of scorpion stings and 184 chicken mite bites on one knee after one night in a village.

Typical Dayak Village House

Then I told them that, like Paul, I had a "deep concern for all the churches" (2 Cor 11:28). I told her about the conflicts we had with other denominations. Their leadership would offer to build our people a new church building, provide them with a fully salaried pastor, and give the pastor a motorcycle. This was powerful stuff when a Dayak would change churches for a free toothbrush! When you have nothing, anything is highly valued. The meetings with the other denominational leaders were always heated. They always made me think about going home. Many of our people were persuaded to leave our fellowship to join with others and then were deeply embarrassed when the others failed to provide the promised aid. Many fell away from the faith because of such things.

I told her of sin in the church and being asked how much a repentant person should be fined before they would be welcomed back into fellowship. I told them of believers who still called the evil spirits when their children were ill, and of pastors who secretly called the shaman to bless their fields before planting or harvesting. I told them of the gullibility and naivety of many who are young in the faith. They were easily deceived by faith healers, and charlatans who promised blessings of healing, health, and wealth in exchange for an offering.

Village Offering to Jubata

I told her of all these things that burdened me and made me want to go home. At home, back in the United States, I could do the Lord's work in greater comfort. I could be near my family and enjoy a higher standard of living.

I told her about my concern for my children. They would need to return to the United States someday. I needed to prepare them for life in their homeland. I needed to prepare for their education—their future. So, yes, I thought about going home. Every day I thought about going home. It would be far easier than staying in West Kalimantan, Indonesia.

"Well," she asked when I finally stopped talking. "Why don't you go home?"

Without hesitation I replied, "Because God has not released me. I cannot go—I will not go—until God releases me from this responsibility to be a light in a dark place. God sent me here, to this place, to these people. He did miraculous things to get me here and to keep me here. I am here to do His work. I cannot, I will not, and I must not leave until He releases me from this work."

Chapter 5

LESSONS LEARNED ABOUT THE CALL OF GOD AND DISCIPLESHIP

My experience of God's call was not, and is not, unique to me. It is the minimum requirement for discipleship. This minimum requirement for discipleship can be called the principle of the cross.

The Principle of the Cross

Consider these two statements by Jesus Christ.

- When He had called the people to Himself, with His disciples also, He said to them, "Whoever desires to come after Me, let him deny himself, and take up his cross, and follow Me." (Mk 8:34).

- And whoever does not bear his cross and come after Me cannot be My disciple. (Lk 14:27).

Commenting on these verses Richard Greene wrote,

> It is through the principle of the Cross that we
> receive and experience the life of the Lord Jesus.
> . . . The term "principle of the Cross" refers to
> the way the Cross works in the life of the dis-
> ciple. It is obvious that when Jesus spoke of the
> disciple taking up his "own cross" He was not
> speaking literally but metaphorically. . . . We
> follow Christ through the daily application of
> the principle of the Cross in our lives. It is as
> I take up my cross that I am a disciple . . . of
> Christ. . . . The principle of the Cross is to give
> one's *life* [italics original], especially to fulfill
> the redemptive purposes of God.[5]

Jesus explained this principle when He taught that
unless a grain of wheat is buried in the earth "and dies,"
it cannot reproduce (Jn 12:24). In the same way St. Paul
stated, "I have been crucified with Christ; it is no longer
I who live, but Christ lives in me; and the life which I
now live in the flesh I live by faith in the Son of God,
who loved me and gave Himself for me" (Gal 2:20).

The principle of the Cross means that a true disciple of Jesus must die to his own will, to his own
plans for his life, and embrace the call of God on his
life. Anything less is not discipleship. If one refuses to
do this, one *cannot* be a disciple of Jesus. As Greene
wrote, "To take up our crosses is to surrender our lives
to God, to live for Him and not for ourselves. The Cross
empowers us to live as those who have died."[6]

It means that Christ, and Christ alone, decides what
our profession will be, who our spouse will be, where

we will live, and how we will live. Christ makes these decisions for His disciple—not the disciple himself, not his fiancé, and not his father. The true disciple, the one who has taken up his cross, has surrendered the power to answer those questions to Christ. This is an essential lesson for the disciple to learn. It is one that St. Paul learned and demonstrated in his life and ministry.

St. Paul's Experience

The Scriptures show us how Paul gave up his purposes in life for the redemptive work of Christ, demonstrating the principle of the Cross in his life and ministry.

By the time Stephen was stoned, Paul had launched a brilliant career for himself. Born in the city of Tarsus to an Israelite family of the tribe of Benjamin (Phil 3:5), Paul was circumcised on the eighth day, in compliance with the law of God (Ge 17:12, Lv 12:3, Phil 3:5). He was sent to Jerusalem for his education. He attended a Pharisaic Rabbinical school and was taught personally by Gamaliel (Acts 22:3). This Gamaliel was a leader of the Sanhedrin, the high council of the Jews (Acts 5:34).

Paul stated that the Pharisees knew his "manner of life" from his "youth" (Acts 26:4). He confidently asserted that he lived "according to the strictness of our fathers' law, and was zealous toward God," and that "the high priest . . . [and] all the council of the elders" could verify this (Acts 22:3–5).

Luke records that Paul was present at the trial and stoning of Stephen. He was so trusted by the Sanhedrin that he was responsible for their coats as they stoned Stephen (Acts 7:58). Further, Paul was entrusted by the Sanhedrin with the task of pursuing the disciples of Jesus. He "received authority from the chief priests" to arrest and imprison the disciples, and he was empowered to vote for them to be put to death (Acts 7:58; 8:1; 26:9–11).

All this demonstrates that Paul had a clear plan for his life. He aggressively pursued political power and influence. He "advanced in Judaism beyond many of [his] contemporaries" because he was "more exceedingly zealous for the traditions of [his] fathers" than his contemporaries (Gal 1:14). This was Paul's plan and purpose for his life—political power and influence as a leader of the Sanhedrin. Everything changed, though, when he met Jesus Christ on the road to Damascus.

God had a different plan for Paul's life. God told Ananias that Paul was "a chosen vessel of Mine to bear My name before Gentiles, kings, and the children of Israel" (Acts 9:15). Paul later reported that God told him:

> But rise and stand on your feet; for I have appeared to you for this purpose, to make you a minister and a witness both of the things which you have seen and of the things which I will yet reveal to you. I will deliver you from the Jewish people, as well as from the Gentiles, to whom I now send you, to open their eyes, in order to turn them from darkness to light, and from the power of Satan to God, that they may receive forgiveness of sins and an inheritance among those who are sanctified by faith in Me. (Acts 26:16–18)

Paul had a choice to make. He had to choose a course of action. Would he renounce his own goals, ambitions, plans, desires, and choices for his life? Would he follow the career path his father had chosen when he sent Paul to Jerusalem to study under the leading Pharisee rabbi of the day? Would he continue to seek personal political power and influence as a member of the Sanhedrin and the chief enforcer of its will?

Or would Paul embrace the principle of the Cross? Would he deny his own personal goals and ambitions? Would he take up his cross? Would he follow Jesus? Would he be a true disciple of Jesus? Paul himself testified to his choice.

"Therefore, King Agrippa, I was not disobedient to the heavenly vision, but declared first to those in Damascus and in Jerusalem, and throughout all the region of Judea, and then to the Gentiles, that they should repent, turn to God, and do works befitting repentance." (Acts 26:19–20)

Paul later wrote to the Philippians that the things he gave up, his own goals and ambitions, were inconsequential when compared to the blessings of knowing Jesus and "the power of His resurrection, and the fellowship of His sufferings, being conformed to His death" so that he "may attain to the resurrection from the dead." (Phil 3:9–11)

My Personal Experience

God's plan for my life was that I would be a prophet to the nations. He prepared me for that calling during my formative years. My father's decision to move the family from his home in Tennessee to Indiana was part of that plan. Dad could not find a job in Tennessee, but he prospered in Indiana. It was in Indiana that he was converted to Christ. This led to his decision to take his family to church whenever the doors were open. What Dad thought to be a terrible thing, being forced to leave his home and family, was part of God's plan to send me as a prophet to the nations.

My training in church began early in life. Because my father forced me to attend church, I learned the Scriptures. These Scriptures did not return void (cf. Is 55:10–11) but accomplished God's purpose. The Scriptures prepared my heart to yield to the call of God and to be a preacher of the Scriptures in obedience to that call.

Yet, I had to make a personal choice to accept God's call and purpose for my life. Like Paul I had a plan for my life. I had goals of my own, things I wanted to be, to do, and to experience. It was my life, and I wanted to live it as I chose. I was a typical American Christian. No one was going to tell me how to live my life!

However, when I accepted Christ, I had to make a choice. I had to decide if I would, like St. Paul, give up my own plans for my life and take up my cross—accept the call of God on my life, and follow Jesus. I chose to follow Jesus.

The call of God on my life held me to the task through many troubles. Through times of extreme financial hardship, I was held to the task by my certainty that God had called me to missions. Through times of extreme physical and emotional hardship, I was held to the task because I knew God had called me to West Kalimantan. It was only when I knew beyond all doubt that God had released me from the ministry to the Dayaks that I could leave Indonesia. The certainty of God's call on my life as a missionary, as a prophet to the nations, and to the Dayaks of West Kalimantan was essential to successful missionary service.

Summary

Discipleship begins at the Cross. Unless one renounces one's own goals and purposes, renounces the demands of one's parents, and renounces the power and pleasure of one's own culture, one cannot be a disciple of Jesus. Even so, unless one embraces the principle of the Cross, one cannot be a disciple of Jesus. The basis of discipleship is to embrace the principle of the Cross, surrendering one's life to the will of God. Without this surrender, one cannot endure the challenges of the missionary life, or of discipleship.

PART 2

The Power of Discipleship

Chapter 6

LEAN TIMES AND THE PRAYER OF FAITH

God allows great crises in the lives of His people because it enables them to learn how to pray, how to trust, and how to glorify His name. Accepting the call of God to take up the cross and follow Jesus is only the beginning of discipleship. The cross grows heavy. Just as it drove Jesus to his knees on the way to Golgotha, it forces the modern believer to bend the knee.

Every disciple must learn that it is only by the grace of God that we live, and move, and have our being. It is only through the grace of God that we receive our daily bread. It is only through the grace of God that we receive eternal salvation. Finally, it is only through the grace of God that we are called to His service, called to walk in His steps, called to make disciples who make disciples. The grace of God is freely given, but it costs all that we have and are. The true disciple learns to lean on God, to call on Him, and to trust Him to provide all that is needed. Job said it best, "Though He slay me, yet will I trust Him" (Jb 13:15).

We were never rich. Dad worked hard and took all the overtime he could get, but the pay was always low in the early days. When my brother and I were old enough to get by at home on our own, Mom went to work in a local factory and things improved. Eventually, Dad got a better factory job, and our financial situation improved even more. In the lean times, though, I learned that if I wanted something I had to get it myself. I had to work, save, and plan. It was just the way we did things.

Bible College

I received my high school diploma from South Side High School on a Thursday evening. I hired into a local factory the following Monday, and my first day on the job was Wednesday. I was making more money per hour than I could ever have dreamed. By my standards, I was rich. I saved all I could, and by the end of the summer, I was able to buy my first car, a 1965 Ford Mustang. It was five years old, but I was proud of it. It was mine. I earned it.

I started college a couple weeks later, but I kept my job in the factory. I went to class in the morning, and I worked the afternoon shift in the factory. I was still living at home, so I was able to save a pretty good stash. Expenses were low. The wages were good. College was preparing me for a life of service to God. OK, I got this! Success breeds confidence. So Carolyn and I decided it was time to marry.

We were committed to a missionary career. We both knew this was God's call on our life together. We just had to work out the details. Carolyn was in nurses' training, and I was in Bible college. I supported us by working in the factory. After Carolyn became a registered nurse and gave birth to our first son, Joshua, I quit my factory job to attend Bible college full time. I also worked as a youth pastor (small salary and good experience) and a school bus driver (never again!). Whenever I could, I did odd jobs to pick up extra cash. Even then, we had plenty. We were not rich, but we had all we needed. We tithed, paid the bills, saved an appropriate amount, and still had cash for fun times. Essentially, we were able to do whatever we wanted. I completed my college training after one year of full-time study.

Missionary Internship

After I graduated from Bible college we moved to Flint, Michigan as part of our training for missionary service. For three weeks each month, I served as a missionary intern at a United Methodist Church. Carolyn was a stay-at-home mom with our son. On the fourth week each month, we attended a training program preparing us to move to a new culture.

The salary was not even half of what we had earned in Fort Wayne. For the first time in my working life and in our married life, we had to count every penny. We were frugal, but we still had to draw from our savings to stay solvent. It was not pleasant, but Carolyn and I knew it was only the beginning of living on very little cash. We saw it as good preparation for a life of ministry. After nine months, the training program ended, and we returned to Fort Wayne to begin our deputation—the process of raising financial support for our ministry in Indonesia.

Deputation

It was September, 1976. The Vietnam War was over. The economy was soft. No one was hiring. I could not find work. No one wanted to hire me once they learned I intended to move to Indonesia as soon as I could arrange the finances. Finally, Carolyn agreed to return to nursing to support us while I worked on fund-raising. Again, income did not match demand, so we continued to draw on our savings.

Fund-raising is a challenging task. I spent my days calling pastors, arranging speaking engagements, scheduling personal interviews, and following up on new contacts—what we now call networking. I did everything I could to share the vision God had given us for the Dayaks of Indonesia and to recruit prayer and financial support for this mission. It was hard work, but it had to be done. Results were very slow in coming, but our savings dwindled rapidly.

We prayed. We labored in prayer. We asked for financial pledges and prayer supporters for our work in Indonesia. We asked for our daily bread. We asked for God's blessing. We learned to live on very, very little. We believed God would provide and answer our prayers. And we prayed!

Pregnancy

Things changed when Carolyn quietly said, "Wayne, I'm pregnant." What should have been a moment of great excitement and joy—the coming of our second child—only brought fear to my mind. How am I going to pay for this? An obstetrician. Furniture. Diapers. Hospital bills.

"Lord," I prayed, "Where are you? Do you see this? What are you doing? Help us, Lord!"

Time passed and nothing happened. How would we get by when Carolyn had to stop working because of the pregnancy? I was worried, troubled more deeply than at any time in my life. I had no idea what to do. So I prayed.

Have you ever waited for the next shoe to drop? I was very nervous. Funds were tight. I needed a job. I looked for work. I took any job I could find. I worked at a car wash. I sold vacuum cleaners door-to-door. Deputation was put on hold. I had to raise the cash for childbirth. But in spite of all my efforts, all my prayers, the money was still only enough to cover the necessities. Our savings were nearly gone. We prayed, and prayed. We trusted God, but I was nervous—afraid of what would happen next.

Surgery

In early 1977, Josh, our first-born, became ill. He was in pain. Carolyn checked him out and found a lump where it was not supposed to be. We had to see the doctor. (Great—a doctor bill!) The news was mixed. The lump was not a major problem. Josh would be fine. (That was the good news!) He just needed surgery to correct the problem. (That was the *bad* news!) We had no medical insurance and no spare cash. The surgery could be delayed without danger, but eventually it had to be done. Well, Lord, what do we do now? I was desperate.

Prayer

One evening I put Josh to bed at his usual time, about seven o'clock in the evening. Carolyn was on a private-duty nursing job, so I had the evening to myself. I sat down with my Bible and began to read and pray. When Carolyn came home at 11:25 p.m., I was still sitting in the chair with my Bible.

Carolyn needed to rest so she went right to bed. I returned to my chair and my Bible. I prayed. I continued to read my Bible, seeking a new word from God—seeking guidance and answers. I wanted a vision. I wanted a voice from Heaven to explain this mess. I wanted to know that God still knew my name! I prayed, and prayed, and prayed. Sitting, kneeling, standing, pacing about the room, then back to the chair. Nothing. Absolutely nothing. N-O-T-H-I-N-G!

I did everything I knew to do: confession, adoration, worship, supplication. I just prayed. God was silent.

When the sun came up, I heard Josh calling for me as he did every morning. I got him up, so he would not wake Carolyn. I changed his diaper, dressed him for the day, fed him breakfast, and greeted Carolyn with an exhausted smile when she waddled into the kitchen and excitedly placed my hand on a bulge in her belly so I could feel the baby move.

My all-nighter in prayer yielded nothing new. I just had to hold on to what God had already told me. I still had one question, though.

"Lord, if you can't provide for us here, in my home-town, in my own country and culture, how are you going to provide for us in Indonesia?"

Answers

A couple weeks passed. I received a phone call offering me a job in a local warehouse. They needed temporary help loading trucks with goods for a retailer's Easter holiday sale. It was good money—more than I had been paid since I left the factory. We had learned to live very, very frugally, so we were able to save enough to pay for the obstetrician and the hospital. But, the temporary job only lasted a couple months. The layoff was coming.

"Now what, Lord?" I prayed.

During the last week of work at the warehouse, I was offered a job at a local factory making pistons for the auto industry. The wage was even higher than at the warehouse! I left the warehouse on Friday and started at the piston factory on Monday. After three weeks at the factory, we could see that I would be able to earn enough to pay for Josh's surgery. I called the surgeon and scheduled the procedure.

At work the next day, I told the man who was training me about scheduling Josh's surgery. This man, who had worked at the plant for more than twenty years, wanted to know why I was doing such a foolish thing.

"My son needs it," I said.

"I know that," he exclaimed. "But if you wait until you have thirty days on the job here the company insurance will cover it."

"No, they won't." I countered. "It's a pre-existing condition. Insurance companies won't cover that."

"Yes, they will!" he asserted. "At lunch time, you just walk into the office and ask about it. You'll see. When you work for this company, they take care of you!"

He was right. I rescheduled the surgery for a date after I had thirty days on the job. I did not have to pay a dime for it.

Soon, Carolyn delivered our daughter, Rachel. My wages were sufficient for Carolyn to stay at home with our kids. We paid the doctor and the hospital with the money we had saved. We even had some savings left after paying all our bills. I took a deep breath of relief and again thanked God for answered prayer. He was proving that He could take care of us in my hometown. My faith was growing. Now, what about the funding for our mission to Indonesia?

I worked the phone with renewed energy. Monday through Friday I made pistons in the factory. Saturday and Sunday I preached missions, cast the vision for the Dayaks, and shared our need for support in finances and in prayer. By September 1977, I had exhausted every contact I had. There was no one left to call and nowhere else to go. We were still significantly short of what the sending agency required us to raise.

"OK, Lord," I prayed, "what do I do now?"

Again, nothing—no vision, no voice, no illumination. Knowing I had done all I could do, I told Carolyn it was just time to go. We would go with what we had and let God take care of us. After our fortunes had changed so dramatically in a matter of months, I was certain that God would provide.

The sending agency applied for our Indonesian visas. Miraculously, they were granted in less than a month! No one had gotten visas for Indonesia in years! (The mission had not told us that before we'd applied.) But now, God opened the door, and we had our visa. We had to enter Indonesia by a certain date, though, or it would be revoked. Short of pledged support or not, we were going to Indonesia.

I was ordained at our home church on December 4, 1977. The denomination reviewed my character, training, calling, and ministry experience. They appointed me as their representative to the Dayaks of West Kalimantan, Indonesia. Further, Rev. Reginald Alford, the pastor of our home church, informed me that the church board had decided to take on responsibility for all our remaining unpledged support. A little before midnight, on December 31, 1977 we left the United States for Indonesia.

Ordination Day

God had answered my prayer. He had shown me that He was able to take care of us. The financial crisis led me to pray. God demonstrated His power, His glory, and His love. I learned how to pray, how to trust, and how to glorify His name. It was essential for what was yet to come.

Chapter 7

LEAVING FOR INDONESIA AND PRACTICING THE PRESENCE

We arrived in Indonesia on January 2, 1978, about 10:30 p.m., after thirty-three hours en route. We had left Los Angeles International Airport just before midnight on December 31, 1977, bound for Honolulu. Our six-hour flight was followed by four hours sitting in the airport. Another six-hour flight took us to Taipei and four more hours in another airport. The flights and waits and loading gates merged into a blur of fatigue, piles of baggage, loading ramps, diapers, baby food— yes, diapers and baby food! Josh was three and a half years of age, but Rachel was only six months old when we left the United States. By God's grace, and in answer to many prayers from us and our prayer team, Josh and Rachel traveled well without major meltdowns or, really, any problems at all. It was just long!

When that plane touched down in Jakarta, all we wanted was sleep! So we gathered our gear (carry-on baggage for two adults, one pre-schooler, and one infant), and headed for the airplane door. As I was walking to the door, I prayed, "Lord, what do I do now?" At that moment it seemed like all the evil of the universe was waiting for me beyond that door. I had no idea what to do once I got beyond that door, and I was afraid. I did not want my wife to know it, though, or my kids, so I whispered that prayer and stepped into the darkness.

The heat and humidity hit me like a slap in the face. Late at night, it was still over 85°F with extremely high humidity. At the bottom of the loading ramp stairway, I waited for Carolyn and the kids, adjusted my load, and realized God had answered my prayer for guidance. There was only one thing I could do—follow the Indonesian folks who had deplaned before us into the building.

Once inside, we were surrounded by the cacophony of a thousand people crammed into space designed for fifty (well, it seemed that way to me). All were screaming at one another, babbling on with eerie, meaningless sounds, while waving their arms or trying to grab my bags out of my hands and my daughter from her mother's arms. Josh had wrapped both arms firmly around my leg, and Carolyn was squeezing Rachel desperately to her shoulder—as overwhelmed as I was. I looked around, trying to figure out what I needed to do and saw a short, grey-haired white man with thick black-framed glasses waving and pointing. For the first time I realized that angels were not always handsome lads in shiny white robes. I quietly offered my second prayer on arrival in Indonesia, "Thanks, Lord!"

A Pattern of Prayer

So began a pattern of prayer that still continues. A silent appeal for guidance from a troubled soul, a practical answer, and a simple expression of thanks when the crisis was over. It was a pattern I used often over the years in Indonesia.

I used it when a truck rear-ended my motorcycle and sent me skidding and rolling down the street with the truck's right-front tire only inches from my face—a tire locked up tight by excellent disc-brakes (amazing what you notice at a moment like that) skidding down that asphalt along with me. When the tire and I both came to a stop, I could count the stones stuck in the tread (there were four). So I rolled out from under the front bumper, staggered back to my feet, whispered, "Thanks, Lord!" and started to breathe again.

I used it again as I stood there wondering, "What does one do in Indonesia when involved in a traffic accident? This was not covered in Anthropology 101!" As I stood there in the midst of a dozen Indonesians laughing and screaming at one another, gesticulating wildly, pointing at me, imitating how I was skidding on the asphalt, I whispered out loud, "Now what, Lord?" I discovered that angels were not always white men.

An Indonesian man came driving through the crowd on his Italian-made motor scooter. He spoke authoritatively to the driver of the truck, and silence settled on the crowd. Words were exchanged. He turned to me and asked—in English, praise the Lord—if I was OK. When I explained that I was OK, he told me I should put my bike in the back of the truck that hit me and they would take me to have it repaired.

Two hours later, with my bike repaired, a huge friction burn on my hip treated by my loving wife, and a delicious cup of *kopi susu* in hand, I put my foot up on the coffee table, rested my head against the back of the metal-framed chair and quietly said, "Thanks, Lord!"

I used that pattern of prayer many times over the thirteen years we devoted to manifesting the glory of God in Indonesia. I used it when confronted by a group of angry Muslims as I was eating in the provincial capital during Ramadan. I used it when I was confronted by a policeman who aggressively told me, "All religions are same, aren't they?" I used it when I fell off a bridge into a river with my motorcycle, and when I had to tread a five-inch circumference tree over a deep chasm in the remote fastness of virgin jungle, two days trek from the nearest medical care. I used it when confronted by a machete-wielding Dayak, angry about a pig I had accidentally killed.

I also used it when I stood before an entire village of Dayaks who had never heard of Jesus Christ. I used it when a local church so insulted their head elder that he refused to serve any longer, and the group wanted to choose an unworthy man in his place. I used it when I had to address fifty Dayak church leaders whose public transport vehicle blew a tire as they came to a training seminar at my station. These leaders had seen their friends scattered across the pavement like matchsticks tossed from the box—every one of them knew that at least one brother was dead, one was paralyzed, and others' lives were hanging in the balance.

In those moments there was no time to fall on my knees, fold my hands, close my eyes, and offer an eloquent prayer. I needed help that only God could give, and I did not need it "later." I needed it *now!* In those moments, God always answered my prayer. Every time. No exception. In every crisis, I knew He would answer. But what about when the need was not a crisis, but a problem simmering like soup on the stove?

A Need for Guidance

My last four years of ministry in Indonesia were joyous and blessed! I was living in Anik but teaching at the local Bible school in Ansang—just two kilometers from Darit in the Manyuke District. I was pastoring a local congregation. I was leading outreach and discipleship operations in two remote areas where trained workers seldom visited and where the gospel was only nominally preached unless I went there. I was blessed with my ministry, finding amazing joy in serving Jesus and these wonderful Dayak people! But a cloud was growing on the horizon. A growing uneasiness troubled my spirit.

Wayne Teaching

147

The cloud was the political situation in Indonesia. There was a growing push by increasingly aggressive Muslim elements, funded by oil money from Saudi Arabia, to end the missionary presence in the country. Our residence visa renewal process was increasingly difficult. Our visas had to be renewed annually. We would finish the process and obtain our new visas just in time to start the process for the next renewal. I could see the end of our ministry coming.

This was confirmed when another family on our team was denied their visa renewal. They left the country and transferred to the Philippines. They were starting over with a new language, a new culture, and a new target group. I knew it would not be long before we would have to face the same challenge. The cloud was growing, and there was another problem.

I gradually came to understand that the Dayaks were not taking responsibility for manifesting the glory of God in their region. They preferred to let me and my missionary colleagues do it. Since we were better at it— better trained, more experienced, better financed, with more contacts, greater vision, and greater gifts from the Spirit (in their opinion)—they thought it best to just let us do it. They could get on with their lives and leave the vital tasks of declaring His glory and making disciples to us. They thought there was no need for them to do anything but to let the professionals do it. It encouraged us to know that the Dayaks recognized our skill, gifting, anointing, and power for ministry; but it did not prepare them for the day when we would be gone and the task was theirs alone. I was very uneasy about the future. So, I prayed, "Lord, what do I do now?" As usual, God answered.

Our denominational magazine arrived in the monthly mailbag. We read through it eagerly. It was news from home, of people we knew, of churches that supported us, and of the work of God in our homeland. Reading through it, I noticed that my alma mater, Fort Wayne Bible College (FWBC), was seeking a new missions professor. I told Carolyn I was going to apply for the position. This wonderful woman, who had supported me and encouraged me through endless troubles, mistakes, joys, and sorrows and who had patched me up from endless cuts, scrapes, and abrasions; who had encouraged me to go to the villages, and to spend weeks working on huge tasks always believing that I would succeed at whatever God would lead me to do—this wonderful woman told me, "Why bother? They are not going to hire you!"

Really, she was right. FWBC was looking for someone with a doctoral degree, or at least a candidate for the degree. They wanted someone who had an established reputation in academia and had published widely. I had a one-year Master of Arts degree and had never published a word. No way were they going to hire me. Still, I had prayed, "Lord, what do I do now?" and here was something I would love to do, in a place we would love to live, at a time when I needed something to do. So, I applied. I sent them a resume. I had never written one before, so I hate to think what it must have looked like. Thankfully, I do not have a copy of it. I had no idea anything would come of it. I had lessons to plan, lectures to prepare, sermons to deliver, villages to visit.

"Carolyn is right," I thought. "They are not going to hire me, so get back to work. You have to help these Dayaks take responsibility for the Gospel." I focused on my work, but the cloud continued to grow and the uneasiness continued to trouble me.

A month later I received a reply. They wanted me to call them to arrange a phone interview. " " I thought. We made the trip to Pontianak. I arranged with a colleague to use his house phone for the interview. Carolyn sat quietly in the room as I answered their questions, shared my thoughts on missions, and struggled to make them understand what God was doing in Indonesia. After the call, I was excited, but Carolyn said again, "They are not going to hire you!" Two weeks later, though, I received a job offer.

A Decision to Make

Again I prayed, "Lord, what do I do now?" I had time to contemplate since this was not one of my normal emergency situations. Yet, I really did need guidance. I had to reply to the offer in a very short time. Carolyn and I talked endlessly about it. We did not tell the kids. We did not tell anyone. We just talked and prayed. My prayer remained, "Lord, what do I do now?"

A part of me wanted to go. It was a chance to go home. My children were getting older. It would be good for them to return to Fort Wayne to establish their own identity in preparation for adult life. It would be good to be back with family and friends, to connect with our fathers before they joined our mothers in glory. It would be good to have running water, hot showers, paved streets, and a steady workweek.

But a part of me did not want to go. These folks were family now. Missionaries, church members and elders, shop owners, and truck drivers—all were dear friends. If I did not go to the villages, who would? Ulu

Tayan and Lokok and Lumar—would anyone ever preach there again? What about those distant villages beyond Ulu Tayan, and who would pastor the local church or teach the courses at the Bible school?

We finally decided it was time to go. I informed FWBC that I would accept the offer. I was uneasy in my spirit, though. I asked myself, "Are you taking this job just to get out of Indonesia? Are you just trying to get out of a tough situation and back to the comforts of home? Are you running away from a tough job just because it is tough?" I was not sure. For the next three days I was troubled by my decision. I knew I could call them before they received the letter and retract the acceptance of the contract. I could not get it out of my mind. Am I running away, or am I following God's call? Almost hourly I was praying, "Lord, what do I do now?"

A Confirmation

Part of our daily schedule in West Kalimantan, Indonesia was the thirty-minute short-wave radio time. From 2:30–3:00 p.m. we signed on to our designated frequency to communicate with the other members of our missionary team. There were no phones available then, and the distances were great. This was the only way we could communicate with our team, short of a two-hour trip over muddy, slippery roads. All the important news was communicated over the short-wave radio. It was my practice to have an afternoon cup of coffee and relax a bit while the radio conversation took place. Carolyn and our colleagues on the station, two single nurses who had served in the area since Noah was a kid, would handle the conversation and let me know if anything important happened.

We were living in Anik then, and on the third day after sending off my acceptance of the teaching contract at FWBC, Carolyn went over to the neighbors' house for radio schedule as usual while I sat down in our front room with a cup of steaming hot *kopi susu*. I gave my attention to reading the current *Time* magazine and savoring my coffee, so I was quite surprised when Carolyn appeared in the doorway, asking why I had not answered her shout-outs across the yard. She explained that our field director had news for me, and I needed to come to the radio immediately.

Well, it is never good news when the boss calls unexpectedly, so I jumped up (quite a challenge with a cup of *kopi susu* in my hand) and headed over to find out what was up. The field director informed us that they had just received our passports back from the immigration office. We had applied for our visa renewal as usual, and our national office manager had just that day picked up our passports.

"You have been granted a six-month extension," my director said, "but your passport visa page has been stamped *'Tidak Boleh Diperpanjang"* or 'May Not Be Renewed.' You have six months to leave Indonesia." While we could return as tourists or on short-term visas, we would no longer be permitted to live in Indonesia. I took a deep breath and whispered, "Thanks, Lord!" I knew what He wanted us to do.

Summary

In those long months as we struggled to fulfill God's calling—when I had no job, no medical insurance, no money—I learned to pray. I spent hours on my knees praying. I spent more hours pacing about the house, walking in the yard, and sitting at the kitchen table reading the Word and praying. I learned to toil in prayer, and I learned to trust Him to answer in His time. Really, I learned to seek the Lord until He answered. This is powerful praying as it changes the pray-er, the one offering the prayer. It makes the pray-er seek God with all his or her heart.

Carolyn and Rachel at Anik Church Farewell

In these life situations I learned to pray in short, whispered ways. I learned to walk in prayer—to be in constant communion with Him, to be listening for his voice, and letting Him guide me into the proper course of action. In short, I learned to practice the Presence.

Both styles of prayer are vital for our Christian living and service. There remains a third type of prayer that is vital for missionary service: corporate prayer. It was my final lesson in Indonesia.

Chapter 8

RACHEL'S ILLNESS AND THE PRAYER OF THE CHURCH

Times of prayer are essential to the Christian life. Practicing the Presence is, too. Both types of prayer are powerful. Corporate prayer is a third type of prayer that plays a powerful role in the life of God's people. God allows great crises in the lives of His people because it enables them to learn how to pray, how to trust, and how to glorify His name. I was about to learn the power of a praying church.

The decision was made. We were leaving Indonesia. I would teach missions subjects at Summit Christian College (the new name for FWBC). Carolyn would revive her nursing skills. Josh and Rachel would learn American culture in preparation for a life in the United States. Caleb, who had just been born at the Conservative Baptist hospital in Serukam, West Kalimantan, would get to meet his grandfathers. We began the preparations eagerly but with deep sorrow. We would leave behind many for whom we cared deeply and with whom we had shared joys and sorrows.

There was much to do. Moving house is a large task that requires careful planning. Moving house halfway around the world is even more complicated. We had it under control until Rachel said the one thing you never hear in the Borneo jungles unless you just finished a five-hour motorcycle ride in a huge rainstorm!

"Mom" she said, "I'm cold."

It was the beginning of fear, and a fight for Rachel's life.

The Illness

Rachel had just returned from the Wednesday evening prayer meeting. She had walked over a half-mile to and from the church on a typical equatorial night of 85°F temps and 85 percent humidity. There was only one reason why she would be cold—fever.

Carolyn asked the usual questions, and sent Rachel off to bed. She then walked across the yard to consult with Aunt Ginny and Aunt Clara. Ginny and Clara were not really "aunts" to any of us, but that was how our children addressed other members of the field team in West Kalimantan. Team members were family— replacing the aunts and uncles back in the United States or Canada that the MKs (i.e., missionary kids) rarely got to meet. Aunt Ginny and Aunt Clara were truly family for our kids after sharing the Anik mission station for over four years.

Rachel with Durian

Ginny and Clara were also registered nurses with years of experience treating the illnesses common to West Kalimantan. Clara had arrived in Borneo before I could walk, and Ginny arrived while I was still in high school. They had forgotten more about jungle diseases than most American physicians would ever know. When someone was cold on a hot Borneo night, Ginny and Clara always knew what to do. So, Carolyn did the best thing she could have done that night—she went to talk to Ginny and Clara.

It was malaria—deadly, but manageable. Just take two pills now, along with two aspirin. Take one pill morning and evening for the next three days. Drink lots of fluids. Rest. In seven days she will be hosting tea parties with her friends in the yard again. No problem. We got this covered.

But the next morning the fever and chills came again, exactly twelve hours later. Well, it is early. She's only had two doses. It sometimes takes a little longer to clear out the plasmodium, the little bug that causes the disease. She will be better tonight. But that night the fever and chills came again, just twelve hours after the second attack—typical malaria progression.

Friday dawned hot and sunny. We waited for the fever to rise, for the chills to begin shaking her body again, all the while praying that it would not happen. I was practicing the Presence as I went about my assignments for the day, teaching Bible and theology at the Bible school, preparing a message for Sunday services, and talking with folks who needed help with spiritual problems. I was practicing the Presence, just asking Jesus to heal my daughter, to ease her pain, and to prevent the next malaria attack, all the while constantly pushing down the fear that was growing in my mind.

I whispered a quiet and desperately disappointed, "Why, Lord?" when the fever spiked higher than ever, and Rachel was no longer able to eat or drink. This was getting serious.

High fever in the tropics can kill in forty-eight hours, sometimes even less. Rachel had not been able to drink for at least twenty-four hours. She needed fluids. So, this expert nursing team set up the IVs. It was home health care, and no one ever had a better team for treating malaria. Ginny and Clara had done this many times. They had defeated this little bug times without number, and they would do it again. But still I prayed that evening. I prayed, and my fear increased.

The Wait

Carolyn spent most of the night sitting at Rachel's bedside, watching the IV, checking on her temperature, urging her to drink, to suck on some more ice cubes, and to eat a little bit.

I waited, and I prayed. I watched darkness descend on the jungle and creep in through the windows. I listened to the cicadas offering their nightly songs of praise to their Creator and prayed for God to heal. I listened to the frogs croaking their rhythmic praises to the Almighty.

Through it all I prayed just as desperately as I prayed that night back in Fort Wayne when I wondered if God couldn't supply our needs in my hometown, then how could He supply in Indonesia. I drew hope from that experience.

I thought back over the years since that long dark night, and I knew God was listening. I knew He was in charge. I knew I could trust Him. I just wanted that next attack not to come. I prayed. I dozed. I woke to ask Carolyn how Rachel was doing. Each time I asked, I just *knew* she would say Rachel had turned the corner. She was improving. But as the sun rose that Saturday morning, so did Rachel's temperature. It went higher than we had ever seen it. The chills shook her body like leaves in the wind. As the light grew, so did my fear.

I was supposed to preach in Bebunting on Sunday morning. It was a quiet Dayak village a few minutes' motorcycle ride away—past the medical clinic where Ginny and Clara had saved so many lives from malaria, across the Menyuke River on a swaying suspension bridge, down the hillside and across the swampy bottom land, up the next hill into the village, and then south to the church building where God's people would be waiting to hear the Word of the Lord. I don't remember what I planned to preach that day. I just remember struggling to put together two rational thoughts when my mind was consumed with fear and hope.

On Saturday night, though, I learned I would not be able to preach in Bebunting that Sunday. I remember vividly the bitter taste of fear when Carolyn told me that the IVs had not worked, the medicines were not working, and we needed to take Rachel to the hospital.

Rachel 1990

I arranged for someone to preach at Bebunting in my place. We loaded up the Toyota Land Cruiser and hit the road. Josh was in Manila, attending Faith Academy, but Caleb was with us. We would not be able to care for him at the hospital, so we left him with a team member family and drove with all possible speed to the hospital.

Speed was impossible, though. The road was a mixture of large rocks and red clay. It was dotted with holes filled with the day's rain. It was slick as ice, so a careless turn of the wheel could send us sliding into the flooded ditch beside the road.

Typical Road Conditions

We bounced over the bumps, the holes, and the deep ruts cut into the mud by daily traffic. Carolyn had placed a mattress on the floor in the back of the Land Cruiser so Rachel could recline during the ride, but it was impossible to protect Rachel from the jarring bounces. Speed was essential, but it only increased her pain. I had to drive slowly all the way to the hospital, but even the rattles from that old Land Cruiser, as it bumped and bounced over the rocks and ruts, could not stop me from hearing Rachel moaning as each bump jarred her body.

It was a four-hour trip through the darkness. All the way, in spite of the demands of driving that vehicle over the rocks and ruts and through the mud, I prayed. With each shift of the gears, and each twist of the steering wheel, I prayed for Rachel's healing. The darkness of that jungle road was matched by the darkness of fear in my mind. My hope was in Jesus, but I longed to see the lights of the hospital shining through the darkness.

The Hospital

It was a good hospital, and it still is today. Founded and operated by Conservative Baptist missionary doctors, they had served us well over the years. They did a second surgery on Josh for us. They saved my life from typhoid fever. They helped Carolyn bring Caleb into the world. It was a good hospital. Bert, Beth, and Dan were excellent physicians.

The doctors were not there, though. Not one of our friends was on campus. All were away somewhere doing something else. Only one Indonesian doctor was present, and he was not excited about being called into the hospital late on a Saturday evening. He told the nurses what to do and said he would come "later."

When the next attack hit Rachel "later" that night, and the nurses communicated the severity of the attack, he came immediately. He had not believed Rachel was as sick as we reported, thinking it was typical parental exaggeration. Now he understood. We were fighting for her life.

The Fight

He started Rachel on stronger medicines, ones that should stop the progress of the little bug that was stealing her life. He started IVs so that her body would have the fluids needed to survive. Then he went home. *He went home!* While we sat by the bed and prayed, he went home. I knew it was the normal procedure. I knew there was nothing more he could do at the time; but the sense of abandonment was overwhelming.

It was just Carolyn and I sitting at her bedside, desperately holding on to our now slim hope that these additional medicines would work. We prayed. We begged! Please, Lord, make them work! Don't let that fever return! She can't survive another attack! We prayed, but when the sun came up, so did Rachel's fever.

The fever was higher than I could imagine. When it hit 105°F, Carolyn and I started applying cold compresses on her back and head. A towel soaked in ice water was placed on her forehead. One was placed on her back, by the right shoulder. Another on her left shoulder. By this time the one on her head was already hot from her body heat, so we replaced it with another soaked in ice water. Take one off, put another one on. Take the next one off, soak it in ice water, wring it out, and put it on Rachel. Do it again. And again. And again. Practicing the Presence with each change. Whispering a prayer with each towel.

I lost count of the number of times I switched the towels. I lost count of the number of times ice was added to the water. I lost track of the time. I just kept changing the towels until the sweat ran into my eyes, and I could no longer see clearly to know where to place the towels. Then, when I was no longer sure if it was sweat or tears, I stood upright, wiped the sweat (or tears) out of my eyes and looked around the room.

Carolyn was out in the hallway talking with the physician. Across the bed from me were three nurses, fine Christian ladies all, just watching me. They were just standing there, watching me. Their faces told me clearly that they had given up all hope.

Beside them was the hospital chaplain, Bapak Otto Kanoh. He was from our area, one of the first to believe in Jesus. He had wrestled with demons and shamans in the early days—back when Aunt Clara was just a rookie. He was a man of God with a strong faith and a tender heart. He was just watching me, and I read the hopelessness in his eyes. It was then I lost all hope. I released Rachel into the Father's hands, convinced that we would be going home without her.

I walked out into the hall to join the consultation with the physician. He explained that this was a virulent form of cerebral malaria. Normal medicines were not working. There was only one thing left to try—a quinine injection. If anything could stop the progress of the disease, it was quinine. However, a side effect of such medication was an increased heart rate.

Heart rates could reach alarming levels very quickly. Rachel's heart might not be able to stand the strain. She had often been troubled by a rapid heart rate. The quinine could kill her before the malaria could. The physician asked what we wanted to do. Carolyn just looked at me. I said, "We have to do it." She agreed. I told the physician, "Do it."

My long night of prayer had not brought the answer for which I longed. The moment-by-moment practice of the Presence had not brought healing to Rachel. This medicine could kill her. At this point I realized there was one more thing I could do.

The timing was right, by God's grace. I was able to talk to my colleagues in Pontianak, the provincial capital, via the MAF short-wave radio. I asked my field director to call my father in Fort Wayne, Indiana. It was just about the time that Dad would be going to church for Sunday morning worship. I told my field director, "Tell him to ask the church, the Harvester Church family, to pray for Rachel's life."

The call was made. Dad told the church. Harvester prayed. The family of God united in prayer for one sick little girl halfway around the world. They also prayed for us, Carolyn and me, as we sat by Rachel's bedside praying and waiting—waiting for the next attack to begin; hoping that it would never come, but fearing that it would. The Body of Christ, the Church at Harvester, prayed.

The next attack never came. *It never came!*

As the sun went down, and darkness filled the room a light dawned in my own heart and mind. It was past time for the attack. For the first time in five days, the attack did not come. I realized that God's power is unleashed when the Church prays.

Lessons Learned About Prayer

I learned to pray in earnest, how to meet God in a powerful, personal way by praying though an economic crisis. I have used that form of prayer many times over the years—at times when I needed God to walk with me, to protect, to provide, and to act. I saw Him answer prayer many times to eliminate problems, overcome evil, and open doors that seemed to be closed. I learned how to call on the name of the Lord and find help in a time of need.

I learned to walk in His presence by calling on Him to guide me in a difficult decision. Walking with Him became a part of my daily life. Whispering to Him my thoughts, my hopes, and my requests opened up a new way of thinking and living. I became cognizant of His presence and learned to draw on his power for all I need moment-by-moment. I learned to hear His voice and to trust Him to guide me. I learned this by facing a crisis.

I learned the power of united prayer by the Body of Christ through the crisis of Rachel's illness. I learned that when the Body prays, mountains are moved, and little ones are restored to their fathers. There is great power in the prayers of the Body of Christ. Each time I share these experiences, lives are changed, people are blessed, and God is glorified.

God allows great crises in the lives of His people because it enables them to learn how to pray, how to trust, and how to glorify His name. We have this power, this great power of prayer, in our minds and hearts. By prayers of faith, we can change lives, eternal destinies—even nations. We can open doors closed to the gospel, whether they are the doors of a resistant heart or an apostate nation. We can open those doors if we pray. If we ask anything according to His will, He hears and He answers.

What are you asking of God? Ask, and it will be given to you. Ask, and He will give you the nations for His kingdom. Ask, and He will give you your family for His kingdom. Ask, and He will make you a witness for His name. Ask for your daily needs—rent money, food, health, safety, and peace with family and neighbors. Ask, and He will give you the desires of your heart as long as they are in line with His will. Ask, and through you, lives will be changed, eternal destinies altered, and nations pulled back from destruction.

PART 3

The Methods of Discipleship

Chapter 9

THE SEKAYAM TREK

The basis of discipleship, of the missionary life, is the principle of the Cross. One must surrender one's own life goals, dreams, plans, hopes, and desires and replace them with those given to you by Jesus Christ. The power of discipleship is prayer. One must learn to communicate with God through prayer, drawing strength from Him for every situation. The methods of discipleship are as varied as the colors of the sunset. My ministry in the Sekayam River valley offers insights into the various methods we used to evangelize the Dayaks of West Kalimantan, Indonesia.

The Cloud

Life during our first two years in West Kalimantan was a continual learning experience. Every day, Carolyn and I learned something new — a new word, a new shop in the market, a trail to a new village, or a new insight into Dayak culture. The list was endless because we had so much to learn. Eventually we came to feel at home in the country and to understand enough to feel comfortable with our new lives. Yet, I could not get rid of The Cloud.

From our first days in Indonesia we entered The Cloud. It was a vast cloud of uncertainty. We never—never—completely understood what was going on around us. In the early days, folks would speak to us in Indonesian, and we would have to translate every word in our minds, consider them as a unit, and then form some conclusion about what was said. If we had the words right and recognized them properly, we could form an idea about what was said. Then we could try to form a reply. It was a slow cumbersome process. It was humbling. Five-year-old children were more fluent than us, and they loved to laugh at our mistakes. We worked hard at language acquisition, and over time our skill in the language improved, but The Cloud remained. There was always this cloud of uncertainty around us. We were always thinking, "Did I understand that right?"

By autumn 1980, The Cloud had retreated to a foggy background to all that we did, but it was still there. We were functional in the language. We knew how to take care of the daily needs of life. We could converse with folks about basic things, and even talk a bit about politics and religion. Of course, we were best at talking religion! But The Cloud was still there.

The Village of Lokok

At this time we were living in Pontianak, the provincial capital. My specific assignment was to prepare cassette recordings that could be distributed to the interior villages for folks to play on cassette players. These machines were ubiquitous by this time. Batteries were readily available but expensive for the Dayaks in the remote areas. RBMU put together a plan to provide cassette players that would operate on solar power or by means of a hand crank. We were tasked with producing cassettes with gospel content to help with the spiritual growth of the folks in the village. I was responsible to write the scripts, record them, duplicate the cassettes, arrange for distribution, train folks to use them, and follow up on the use of the machines and recordings. It was a big job, but it had tremendous potential.

Another part of my job assignment at the time was to oversee evangelism and discipleship in the remote areas of the province. Every male team member was assigned a specific remote region within our national church's sphere of influence. Our national church was the PPIK. It was divided into ten districts. All the districts were led by a district board consisting of a director, assistant director, treasurer, and secretary. These were all Dayak men residing in the districts they served. They were chosen by a vote of representatives from the local churches in the districts. A resident missionary helped to lead Districts 1, 2, 4, 7, 8, and 10. Districts 3, 5, 6, and 9 did not have a resident missionary, so the other missionaries were assigned to assist the national leadership there. I was assigned to District 9.

District 9 was Lokok. Lokok is a mountainous region near Mt. Niut, near the border with Malaysia. There were two ways to reach Lokok—by road or by air. By road, there were several options.

I could take public transportation to Ngabang, which would take four or five hours. Then I could catch a boat heading up the Landak River to Serimbu. This took two to four days depending on water level, rainfall, engine repairs, and so forth. Or I could walk from Ngabang to

Serimbu—a twelve-hour trek. After spending a night in Serimbu, I could head west to Lokok—another twelve hours of walking through the Borneo jungles.

I could also walk in from the west or from the south, but it still would take two full days of walking to get there. Alternatively, I could take an MAF flight from Pontianak and be there in forty-five minutes. I always took the MAF flight.

Visiting Lokok was worth the effort, though. It was a great place to visit. We landed on the MAF airstrip constructed on the side of a tall mountain. The pilot of the Cessna 185 would circle the strip to check it out before landing, making sure there were no obstacles on the landing strip. Once certain that all was well, he would circle out to the east to line up his approach. It was always a spectacular landing—at least to me. We flew right at the side of the mountain, pulling the nose up at the last minute, touching down, and immediately gunning the engine so it would not stall as it climbed up the mountainside to the staging area on the crest.

Every landing there reminded me of what the pilot said to me after my first flight with MAF. On that occasion, we had landed on the smooth, even strip in Menjalin with absolutely no difficulties. I was sitting in the front seat beside the pilot. I was totally fascinated by all that went into landing that plane on the narrow strip of grass and then taxiing up to the staff house. At the end of the strip, the pilot executed a slick 180-degree turn to prepare for takeoff and then shut down the engine. My relief that it was over must have shown on my face. Looking me right in the eye he quietly stated, "Well, we cheated death again."

Yep, every time I landed at Lokok, I remembered his words—and often repeated them in a whispered prayer of thanksgiving. My prayers were encouraged after I heard that one of the pilots had crashed his Cessna into a bamboo grove on the side of the mountain. The bamboo was all that prevented it from dropping a couple thousand feet to the river gorge below. Of course, my relief at the successful landing was always tempered by the knowledge that I had to fly out of there in a couple days. That was strong motivation for my prayer life. Yes, it was!

Beyond the excitement of the landing at Lokok, there was the joyous reception we always received. Suarno, the pastor, lived in a small house behind the church on the south side of the airstrip. Suarno had been assigned to Lokok by someone—I never knew if it was a missionary or a national church leader—but he had been there for a couple years when I began visiting. He was a fine Dayak Christian, dedicated to the Lord and committed to serving wherever God sent him. His wife and two children were delightful folks. The isolation was hard on them though, so when we arrived for a visit their excitement was palpable. They were just glad for someone to share a cup of coffee and good conversation with them, to pray with them, and open the Bible for spiritual refreshment. Their excitement at our arrival just made it a great day.

Of course, we always arrived with a couple pounds of sugar, coffee, and tea. We usually took along a case of canned sardines in tomato sauce, and a case of packaged noodles. When we could, we also took along some salted fish. They could not get these things locally. As I said, it was a full day's walk out to Serimbu—which was the nearest place they could buy coffee, sugar, tea, sardines, noodles, and salt fish—so they did not make the trip very often.

Personally, I always took a case of sweetened condensed milk so I could have my *kopi susu* while there. Suarno loved it as much as I did, and we shared many a long, sleepless night talking about the things of God because we both had a strong cup of *kopi susu* after coming back from preaching in a nearby village. We knew if we drank it, we would be up all night; but who can resist *kopi susu* and a long night of talking over the things of God, village life, and how we were going to reach that next village with the gospel—all under a cloudless, starry sky, unblemished by human lights, declaring the glory of God for all who were awake to see it.

Waking up was never a problem, though—even if we talked until the sun was peeking over the mountains. I could never sleep for more than a couple hours at a time. You see, we slept on grass mats spread on the floor. Now, these were fine Dayak-made grass mats, but they have all the sleeping comfort of a sheet of linoleum. There was no cushioning at all. After my first two visits there, I made it a practice to take a hard foam mattress I could roll up and attach to my backpack. It was a good idea, but, really, just wasted effort. Why?

Have you ever seen a floor made of un-planed lumber cut from huge trees with a gigantic backsaw or a chainsaw? Straight lines and even-sized boards are easier to draw than to cut. No two boards are ever the same thickness. What's more, the wood is cut the same day the tree is felled; there is no time to age or dry the lumber. The tree is brought down, the branches are pruned off, the trunk is squared up, and the boards are carried back to the house site when the men go home for supper at nightfall. The next day the boards are on the floor, secured by rattan tie-downs that leave gaps in the floor that make sweeping easy—no need for a dustpan, just let the debris fall through the cracks.

Over time, as the wood dries, the size differences become even more pronounced. One board can be two or three inches higher than the ones beside it. No two boards are level. It is impossible to find a comfortable place to sleep on a grass mat placed on these floors. So, even after staying up all night drinking coffee and talking about the things of God, it was impossible to sleep for more than two hours. By then, the sharp edges of the boards were painful reminders that I was not on my comfortable bed at home.

Still, morning in Lokok was a thing to be remembered! After crawling out of my mosquito net, I would gather up my shaving kit and towel and go *mandi*. Remember, this is the Borneo jungle, just a few miles north of the equator. It is tropical jungle. High temps (85–100°F) and high humidity (85–90%) were just part of life. Even in the early morning, when the mist was still rising from the springs and streams, it is 75–80°F. Remember, too, this is Lokok—about 5,580 feet above sea level.[7]

The *tempat mandi*, the place where one bathes, was about 100 yards down the mountain side from the house. Getting down there was a challenge. Suarno had cut steps into the red clay of the trail to make it easier for his wife to carry water up to the house; but with nearly 200 inches of rainfall annually, these steps rapidly eroded. They became mere indentations on which to pin your hopes for a foothold as you made your way down to the bamboo pipe bringing water in a steady stream from the mountain spring. Getting down there was a challenge, as I said; but getting back up was even tougher. It was similar to climbing Jacob's ladder (Ge 28:12). By the time you made it back to the house, you were covered in sweat and needed another *mandi* — and a good cup of coffee to recover your energy!

Everyone always knew when the missionaries were taking a *mandi*. Let me explain about a *mandi*. Dayaks, like most Indonesians, do not take baths or showers. They *mandi* in the *kamar mandi*, the room where one or takes a *mandi*. A *kamar mandi* has three things: a large water tank with a strong flow of incoming water, a large dipper, and a very efficient drain. When one mandis, one fills the dipper with water and pours it over one's head. It takes about five dippers to get thoroughly wet. Then one applies the soap. When appropriately soaped, one then pours another ten dippers of water over the head to rinse away the grime and soap. That is how you take a *mandi* in a civilized Dayak village. Only the finest Dayak homes have a *kamar mandi* though. Most of them just head for the river. There is always plenty of water in the river!

Suarno's house in Lokok did not have a *kamar mandi*. Instead, we had spring water flowing down a bamboo pipe. It was beautiful water. Clear and clean, we could drink it right from mountain. All other water had to be boiled before drinking, but we could drink this right from the pipe! It was the only cold water for two days in any direction. It was very refreshing after walking back from a village service. It was refreshingly cold on a very hot day.

The water is delicious to drink on a hot day but a great challenge on a cool morning after two hours of sleep in a hot, Dayak house. (Well, Dayaks never leave the shutters open—the night chill might come in and give you a cold or the flu. Or a spirit might come in to steal one of your seven spirits. So it stays hot in the house.)

So how did everyone know when the missionary was taking a *mandi*? When we stepped into that flow of cold water, the scream just naturally roared forth. It was cold! They could hear us scream all the way down the valley! I know because they used to tease me about it.

"What were you yelling about this morning, Pak Pendeta?" they asked. "We heard you all the way down here!"

"It was that cold water! I had to scream to take my mind off the cold!" I replied.

"Wimp," they teased. "We never scream, but you Western guys always do."

He was right. Suarno and his wife never screamed. I did, though, and so did most of my colleagues who visited Lokok with me.

The Sekayam River Valley

During one of my visits to Lokok I heard about the Lokok Christians' outreach to the Sekayam River valley. The Sekayam River was a few miles north of Lokok, running northwest to southeast along the Malaysian border for several miles before turning south to head for the Kapuas River, eventually reaching Pontianak. My friends in Lokok told me that the villages on the Sekayam River had been visited in the past, but it had been many years since anyone had gone there to preach the gospel.

Since my assignment was to minister the gospel to the region, and the Sekayam villages were part of the Lokok ministry region, I determined to visit those villages. It seemed like a natural part of what God had called me to do. I was there to preach and to teach folks how to be good Christians. Sekayam was part of my assigned region. So, I concluded, it was my responsibility to go to Sekayam.

I prepared as best I could. I asked questions about everything! How do we get there? How many villages are there? What Dayak dialect do they use? How many profess Christ? Are there any churches? Are there any Christian leaders there—elders, evangelists, or pastors? Who leads the Christians there? Do they have regular services, or do they just gather when a minister visits? My questions were endless and repetitive.

The Cloud was a serious problem. I was asking questions in my poor Indonesian. The Lokok folks had to process my question into their local dialect and then translate their answer back into Indonesian. Their Indonesian was better than mine, but it was not their first language. They struggled with it almost as much as I did. Suarno was a great help. He was more fluent than any of us in Indonesian, and he had a basic understanding of the local dialect. After two years there, he was an expert as far as I was concerned. Eventually, I thought I had enough information to form a plan.

I would return to Lokok in one month with a medically-trained colleague who would make the trip with us. Church leaders from Lokok would guide us through the jungle, across the rivers, and over the mountains to the Sekayam River valley. We would visit three villages: Suruh Tembawang, Suruh Engkadok, and Tamang (Those are the names as I recall them now, thirty-four years later). We would spend a night in each village. We would conduct our usual village ministry of preaching, teaching, medical work, and general visitation to encourage folks to hold fast to their faith in Jesus. We would start at the northwestern-most village, Suruh Tembawang. We would ask folks there to use one of their boats to take us down river to Suruh Engkadok, and then on to Tamang. After ministry in Tamang, we would travel upriver back to Suruh Engkadok to spend another night in ministry. Then back to Suruh Tembawang for a final night in the valley. The next morning, we would trek back to Lokok. I would arrange for an MAF flight to pick us up at Lokok the following morning. Everyone agreed it was a workable plan and were eager to make the trip.

The Trek

MAF delivered my colleague, Jim, and me to Lokok a month later, as planned. We arrived on Saturday. We preached in Lokok on Saturday night and twice on Sunday. On Monday morning, we set out for Sekayam.

Now The Cloud began to manifest its power. First, Suarno was not going with us. I was certain he had said he wanted to make this trip. The whole idea started with him telling us about the spiritual hunger in the Sekayam River valley. He now affirmed that he could not go. He needed to remain in Lokok to care for the local church and lead services on Wednesday. Since we were planning on six days for the trip, we might not be back in time for Sunday services. Thus, it was imperative that he remain in Lokok. I still do not know how I could have misunderstood him on this, but he was adamant. He insisted he told me from the beginning that he would not make the trip. I do not think my Indonesian was that bad or The Cloud that thick. I think he was scared.

We planned to head out at six o'clock in the morning It would be cooler in the early morning and give us more time to reach our destination before dark. It was a fearsome thing, the Dayaks all affirmed, to be overtaken by darkness while still on the trail. So, Jim and I were up with the sun. We had our morning scream—I mean *mandi* —and our *kopi susu*. We even had fried eggs with our rice and chicken. Mrs. Suarno wanted to be sure we had plenty of energy for our long walk.

After breakfast we reviewed our supplies. Food, water, clothes, medicines, Bible, song book, mosquito net, shaving kit, rain gear—we had it all covered. The backpacks were closed up, and the loose ends secured. We were ready to roll. Now, as soon as the Dayak leaders arrived, we would start. Again, The Cloud interfered.

Departure time came and went, but our colleagues did not appear. It did not matter how many times we looked up the airstrip to the where the trail disappeared into the jungle, no one emerged. We waited. Impatient and bored, we waited. An hour passed. Finally, at 7:30 a.m. we heard the team hail us as they emerged from the jungle. Our questions were met with blank stares. They assured us they had told us from the beginning we would depart at eight o'clock in the morning. OK, I guess I just misunderstood. The Cloud was working overtime. After prayer, we finally started out.

We were a four-man team. Both Jim and I were new in Kalimantan. I was in my third year, and Jim was in his second. We were relying heavily on our Dayak guides, Mustafa and Caming. They knew the trails to Suruh Tembawang. They had walked around these mountains and through these jungles all their lives. So Jim and I trusted them to guide us to our destination. We also assumed they would bring along any necessary equipment for passing through the jungle.

We headed north. Mustafa took the lead. I followed him, with Jim right behind me. Caming brought up the rear. The sun was already hot, and we were covered in perspiration before we had crossed the airstrip and entered the shade under the giant trees of the rainforest.

This was real, original, virgin Borneo rainforest. Some of the giant hardwood trees were over six feet in diameter. The jungle canopy was tens of feet above us. Very little sunshine reached the ground, so it was relatively cool. We joked that it was one of the few places in the world where the temperature and humidity were equal—both at 85°F!

I loved the quiet of the jungle. It was peaceful and reassuring. It was, in my mind, like walking in the Garden of Eden. Well it would have been except for three things—the muddy trail, the dangerous branches of the jungle, and Jim's constant talking.

The average rainfall in Lokok was between 120 inches and 180 inches per year—ten times the average rainfall back home in Indiana. The trails under the jungle canopy never got dry. The mud was just an ordinary part of the trek. The trail was slippery and treacherous. A careless step could send you sliding down the mountainside or have you sitting in a mud puddle while your companions laughed until they cried.

I learned how dangerous the loose limbs and dead-falls could be while we were walking across a newly cleared dry rice field. The Dayaks practiced slash-and-burn agriculture.[8] In July and August each family would identify a place to make its rice field. All trees and brush on the land would be cut down. The good trees would be used for lumber and firewood, the rest would be allowed to dry for a couple weeks. When the wood was sufficiently dry they would set the field on fire, burning off all the bushes, grass, and leaves from the felled trees. Trails would be cut through the by slicing off branches that blocked the way, leaving the stump of the branch jutting out into the air.

We were walking through such a rice field when Jim screamed. This was not a cold scream, but a scream of pain. I turned to see him holding his hand over his right eye, clearly in pain. We gathered round him, asking what was wrong. He explained he had walked into the pointed end of a tree branch. It was high enough that any Dayak would pass under it without difficulty. Even I had passed it by just tilting my head to one side. Jim was taller than us, and he had not seen it. He walked right into it, and sharp point of the branch hit him in his right eye. When he removed his hand we saw that the eye was uninjured. He had a long scratch on the eyelid, but the eye itself was untouched. We gathered around Jim to offer a prayer of thanks that he was not seriously injured and to ask God for further protection as we continued on our way.

Resting at the Rock

By midday we were tired, completely soaked from perspiration, thirsty, and hungry. At the crest of a mountain ridge, in the midst of thick jungle, we found a huge rock jutting up from the ground. It was unique in that it was the only visible rock anywhere around. It stood more than five feet out of the ground. It was smooth and cool to the touch. We decided it was a good place for lunch. Why? I do not know, really. We were in the shade of the trees, and there was a gentle breeze blowing over the mountaintop, so it was cool. It just seemed a good place to take a break.

Mustapha and Caming had brought rice and vegetables wrapped in banana leaves for the trip. They eagerly squatted beside the rock, opened the banana wrappings and began to eat. Things were not so simple for Jim and me.

After much debate, we decided to share a can of cheese and a package of crackers. I handed the can to Jim while I searched for my can opener. When I realized I had not brought one, I asked Jim to get his. Tossing me the can, he searched through his pack. Soon he discovered that he had left his behind, as well.

"Mustapha," I said, "Let me use your machete to open this can of cheese."

"Sorry, Pak Pendeta," he replied, "I did not bring one."

"Caming, can I use your machete?" I asked.

"Pak Pendeta, I did not bring one, either" he said.

I was amazed. I thought Dayaks always carried machetes when they went on the road in the rainforest.

So, how do we open a can of cheese without a can opener or a machete? Break it open with a rock? There were no rocks about, except for the big one jutting up out of the ground.

OK, throw it against that big rock until it breaks open. Sure, that will work. Jim wound up like a baseball pitcher and threw that can of cheese with all his might. It smashed onto the rock and bounced off at a crazy angle—nearly hitting Mustafa in the face as it flew into the jungle. Mustafa leapt out of the way and went to stand beside Caming. Both men were struggling to control their laughter, not wanting to embarrass us. When I started laughing, they both began to laugh out loud.

Undeterred, Jim plunged into the jungle to find that can of cheese. He returned and ordered us to one side as he wound up for a second pitch. Once again, it bounced off at a crazy angle, nearly hitting Mustafa as he now stood on the other side of the clearing.

New peals of laughter filled the air as Jim searched for the can in the brush. Emerging with the can, we both examined it carefully, searching for a break in the metal though which we could extract the cheese. Nothing. Not one crack was to be found. The can was dinted and bent out of shape, but there was no crack.

Now I tried throwing the can. I backed up for a running start, like a cricket fast-bowler. All I achieved was to make the can bounce farther into the brush—and make Mustafa and Caming laugh harder than ever! I tried again. Then a third time. Still not one slight opening in the can.

Jim and I then took turns throwing the can at the rock. After each try we searched for a crack in the tin can. Our frustration grew in equal proportion to our friends' laughter.

Eventually, we discovered a crack in the tin can. It was a tiny little crack, but it was a crack! Now, we just needed something to jam into the crack to pry it open. We needed a knife blade, but no one had a knife. We searched our gear again, but all we could find was a small nail file attached to my fingernail clippers. We shoved that nail file into the can, gradually enlarging the crack to a small hole though which we were able to pry out the cheese—with the nail file.

We devoured the cheese eagerly, as we were now very hungry. The crackers were eaten, too. All was washed down with the water we carried from Lokok. Refreshed, invigorated, and still laughing at our foolish neglect to bring can opener or knife, we resumed our journey.

It was not until well after the trip was over that I told Jim the last thing I did with that nail file before we left Lokok was clean the debris from beneath my toenails.

Resting in the River

Cheese and crackers is a salty meal. Trekking over jungle mountains in tropical heat is thirsty work. Soon our water was finished. After seven hours on the trail we were hot, soaked in perspiration, and thirsty; and we still had three more hours to go. We began to think about a place to rest and refresh for the last stage of the journey.

When we came to a mountain stream, we knew it was time to take a break. The stream rushed down from the mountains, throwing up a fine mist as it bubbled over the rocks. Laying our gear aside, Jim and I waded out to the middle of the stream and sat down on the rocks. The water rushed past us with such force that it was hard to stay on the rocks. The cold water was refreshing and inviting.

All morning we had been drinking the hot water we put in our canteens before we left Lokok. Now, this cold water offered a refreshing change. We recalled King David's longing for a drink of the cold water from the well by the gate at Bethlehem (1 Chr 11:17–18). After confirming that we had a good supply of antibiotics, we both drank our fill straight from the river, and then we were back on the trail to Suruh Tembawang.

Chapter 10

SURUH TEMBAWANG

Our arrival brought great excitement to the village. We were the first Western men ever to visit them. Americans did not just drop in unannounced in this remote village. It was totally unexpected and cause for celebration. The older children came running to greet us—laughing, pointing, and staring at these strange, light-complected giants who suddenly emerged from the jungle.

Caming inquired of them where to find the home of the village headman, and the children eagerly showed us the way. We led a grand procession through the village. Word spread rapidly as the children raced about shouting the alarm that *orang barat* (men of the West) were coming, and soon everyone who could walk was following in our wake to the headman's home.

The good gentleman had been alerted to our coming, so he was standing on the veranda to welcome us. We were ushered into his *kamar tamu* (receiving room, parlor) and welcomed with hot coffee, sweet crackers, and Marie biscuits. Caming introduced us, explained our purpose for visiting, and presented our papers as required by village *adat* (custom) and governmental policy. The headman offered us a gracious official greeting and extended an invitation to conduct our activities in his home during our stay in the village.

As we chatted with the headman, the windows and doors filled with faces eager to see the guests. People of all ages, little ones still carried in big sisters' *selendong* (a long piece of cloth used as a shoulder sling to carry infants), and toothless grandmothers with red-stained lips, watched all we did with eager eyes and wide smiles. Everyone was excited and wanted to see these orang barat. Every move was closely monitored and cause for great giggles. It was evident we would have a huge crowd for the evening meeting.

Accommodations and Arrangements

After much talk, and two cups of coffee, we were escorted to another house where we could arrange our mosquito nets, our sleeping mats, and store our belongings before heading to the river to *mandi*.

The children gladly showed us the way to the river. As we bathed, they splashed about in the water, squealing and shouting as children all over the world will do when they have a chance to jump in the water on a hot day.

Refreshed and clean we returned to the headman's home for our evening meal. Boiled chicken and rice! Delicious! We offered to purchase the chickens, but the headman declined. The village was glad to host us and looked forward to having us as their guests for a couple of days.

The meal was served in typical Dayak style. We were seated on grass mats on the floor. Metal dishes filled with small pieces of boiled chicken were placed in the center of the mats, with large bowls of steaming rice placed at each end. Glasses of steaming water were set before each of us. At the invitation of the headman, we gathered around the feast. The village youth filled our plates with rice, added the best pieces of chicken and handed us our plates. Jim and I were offered spoons, but everyone else just used their fingers to eat.

As we ate, Jim and I kept Caming busy interpreting our questions to the headman and to the village leaders who joined us in the meal. We talked about the history of the village, the state of the rice in the fields, the price of rubber, and the difficulty of transporting the raw products to market. I specifically asked about their tribal stories regarding the origin of the village, when it was founded, where the villagers came from when they moved here, and where their ancestors came from. Did their people come from the northern Sarawak areas or did they migrate up from the Kapuas River valley?

More importantly, I asked about how closely they followed the traditional Dayak rice cycle. Did they offer the seven required blood sacrifices? Did they have a resident shaman who performed the sacrifices? How many heads of families in the village professed faith in Jesus? Did these families participate in the traditional sacrifices? Did the Christians meet regularly, and where did they meet? Did they have a Christian teacher? Who led the meetings? Who did the preaching and teaching? Were any trained to share their faith with others?

Jim asked about the medical care in the village. Did they have a clinic? Did medical personnel visit on a regular basis? Did they have access to basic childhood vaccinations? Where did they get medicines for parasites, infections, gastrointestinal problems, and malaria? What did they do in cases of severe injury, like being hit by a falling tree or a slashed thigh due to a deflected machete swing?

All were eager to talk about their lives in the village, their hard work in the jungle, and the lack of schools and medical care. They were more concerned about the natural things than they were about the spiritual things, but they were eager to receive anything we could offer them to improve their lives. They were very happy that someone, especially *orang barat* were concerned about them.

We discussed our travel plans with the village leaders. They readily agreed to our request to hold a meeting for the village that evening, so I could preach the gospel. They were eager to hear Christian teaching, as it had been years since anyone had visited them. They knew the basics of the faith, and many had "become Christians," but few knew more than the basics.

They also eagerly agreed to allow Jim to conduct a medical clinic in the morning. They would help organize things so that Jim could receive and treat patients in the headman's *kamar tamu*. On the veranda, Caming and Mustafa would screen those who came so that the seriously ill could get priority attention.

At midday, they would serve us another good meal, help us load up a riverboat, and send us on our way. A young village man, Gani, was willing to take us downriver as we had planned. He would prepare for the trip while we treated the sick. He was eager to travel with us to Suruh Engkadok and Tamang.

Preaching the Gospel

After folks returned from the fields and ate supper, they gathered at the headman's house. When we returned there, after resting for a few minutes and praying together, we found the room filled with folks eager to hear what we had to say. The veranda was full, too. Even the windows were full. Many were even peeking through the gaps in the split bamboo walls. We had a great crowd! The headman gave a few words of greeting and invited us to proceed.

Caming led the meeting in a few songs, performed Dayak style. Dayak church singing was similar to dirges sung at funerals in the United States. It was understandable, since few churches had songbooks, and fewer still had musical instruments. Caming did his best, but it was clear the folks were not really interested in what he had to say or in his singing. After a short time, he invited Jim to greet the people.

Village Musicians

Jim gave a brief word of greeting and shared a bit of his personal testimony. Then he invited them to sing again. He purposely selected a song with a fast tempo. Soon the crowd was laughing, singing, clapping hands, and having a grand time. He led the crowd in several songs, all with a fast tempo and all praising Jesus. Then he invited me to present the Word of God.

I gave a simple gospel message, one that I had presented many times and would use many times again over the subsequent years. I began with the creation story, explaining that Adam and Eve were created to live forever in perfect harmony with God and nature. I explained how Eve was deceived by the serpent, ate the forbidden fruit, and gave some to her husband, Adam. I explained that Adam, knowing full well that he was forbidden to eat that fruit and what would happen if he did, ate the fruit.

Wayne Teaching

I explained how they immediately recognized their sin and tried to cover the results of it by using leaves for clothes and hiding from God. I told the story of their confrontation with God, their confession, their punishment, and the promise of a coming child of Eve who would restore to humanity all the blessings that had been lost.

I explained how God provided a better covering for their sin. The blood of an animal was shed to cover their spiritual nakedness, and the skin of that animal covered their physical nakedness.

I explained God taught Adam and Eve to communicate with Him in a new way—through a blood sacrifice—until the promised child came to put all things right. I explained that God continued to work with humanity through the ages so all would be able to communicate with Him and know His love for them. When humanity became too evil for God to allow them to continue, He destroyed the race with a flood and started over with Noah and his family.

When humanity again forgot God's laws, He selected one nation to receive the Truth and to be responsible to pass it on to all nations and tribes on earth. I explained that this nation was the Jews, the physical descendants of Abraham.

Through the history of Israel, humanity was taught five basic truths:

1. There is one God, who is Creator and Ruler of the universe.
2. Humanity has turned away from God, forfeiting His blessing and bringing on themselves God's fierce anger.

3. God sent messengers, through the descendants of Abraham, to tell the nations about Him and His plan to deliver all people from His anger.
4. Jesus was the child promised to Eve. He was sent to open the way for all people to be restored to friendship with God, transforming them from people to be punished into people to be blessed.
5. Those who commit their lives to Jesus become his followers and walk in his ways as revealed in the Bible. They become children of the Creator and inherit eternal life.

It was a lot to teach in one message. Even though I spoke for over an hour, it was hard to explain these things. My purpose, though, was to present the general theme, the outline, showing how the world began, why bad things happen to people, why there are evil spirits around them, and how they can have power over those evil spirits both in this life and in the life to come. I cast a vision for a better life and a brighter future through a personal relationship with Jesus Christ.

I spoke in Indonesian. The villagers understood most of it, but Indonesian was not their heart language. They had questions. They wanted to talk about it. They needed to talk about it. After I ceased speaking, hot sweet tea was served to all present. I chatted with the village headman in Indonesian. Mustafa and Caming chatted with the villagers in their local dialects. Soon, no one was talking to me or Jim. All were talking with Mustafa and Caming in dialect. Jim and I quietly watched as our Dayak brothers led many into the Kingdom of God.

Treating the Sick

When morning came, Jim and I were tired and sore. We had slept little on our beds of grass mats on uneven, un-planed wood plank floors. Mosquitoes, mites, scorpions, and centipedes made their regular visits—not all in one night, of course—but these were our regular visitors whenever we trekked into remote villages like Suruh Tembawang. Nonetheless, a bright sun was shining, coffee was brewing, and a new day was waiting. People were coming for medical help. Jim had promised to use his medical skills and small supply of medicines to help those in need. There was work to do, and we had to get ready.

There was a large crowd waiting for us when we returned to the village headman's home. The veranda was filled with the sick, the elderly, the young mothers and their children, and the curious who just wanted to see what the foreigners were going to do. If nothing else, Jim and I broke the monotony of village life and brought a little excitement for all to enjoy.

Jim and I set up in the headman's *kamar tamu*. Grass mats were again spread on the floor so Jim and I could receive patients. Jim would interview them and decide what was to be done. I would dispense the medicines— liquids, pills, or ointments. Jim would administer the injections. It was fascinating, amusing, and disheartening—all at the same time. No matter what village we visited, the same stories, illnesses, and problems were presented. These are only representative samples of the types of cases presented.

A young mother presented her infant who stopped nursing and had a very high fever. Learning the infant was only a couple weeks old, Jim examined the child's umbilical cord. The green coloration around the belly button revealed that the grandmother had applied the traditional village folk medicine to the belly button. A certain leaf is chewed by the grandmother, removed from the mouth and applied to the cord. It is believed to aid in healing, but what it often does is pass infectious diseases to the child. Antibiotics were given, but there was little hope of saving the child's life.

A little boy presented with a swollen belly and scrawny arms and legs. He was listless and refused to eat. He cried whenever he was forced to eat, and soon vomited up what had been forced down. He was given medicine for parasites, vitamins to strengthen him, and his parents were taught about sanitation—especially the dangers of pig manure.

A young man presented with a mild fever, a runny nose, and a wet productive cough. It had persisted for a couple weeks. He was given antibiotics, aspirin, and advised to rest and take lots of fluids.

A young husband presented his clearly embarrassed wife. He complained she did not get pregnant. He went into great detail about their efforts and how frustrated he was that this woman did not conceive. The poor girl wiped away tears of shame, knowing that the crowd would spread this information far and wide. The husband was oblivious to his wife's physical condition. She was emaciated. If she were to conceive in her malnourished state, it was doubtful if mother or child would survive. Jim sent them away with instructions about improved nutrition, the need for protein, for meat and vegetables, and for fresh fruit—and amounts in excess of what was needed for her daily work in the rice fields. We dispensed pills for parasites, as well.

Another man presented with fever and chills. He was sent away with pills for malaria. He was told to take all the pills as scheduled, two every morning and every evening until they were gone. Also, he should drink and rest.

Another woman presented with clear indications of a bronchial infection. She was given enough antibiotics for two weeks. She was told to take all the pills as scheduled until they were all consumed. We knew, though, that she would take them for a few days until she felt better. Then she would stop, saving the remainder of the pills for the next illness. She would not understand why the illness returned the following week.

A man presented himself for treatment.

"What do you want, sir?" Jim asked.

"I want medicine." he replied.

"Why are you asking for medicine?" Jim asked.

"Because I am sick."

"What is your sickness?"

"My body is sick."

Confused, Jim tried again.

"What part of your body is sick, sir?" Jim asked.

"My whole body is sick! I want an injection to make me healthy!" he replied with a wide smile while waving his hand from head to toe as he was seated on the mat in front of Jim.

Frustrated Jim turned to me and said in English,

"This guy just wants an injection. He thinks everyone is getting one so he wants one, too."

"So what can you do, Jim?" I asked.

"I don't know." Jim replied. "I don't want to waste the medicines I have. I need to keep them for those who are really sick."

"Well," I said, "he is not going to go away without something. He will think you just do not want to help him. You can try explaining he is not sick and you want to save your supplies for someone who really needs it, but he will not be happy. It could get ugly. He could get really mad."

"You're right. He will not take 'No' for an answer."

Jim thought for a moment and then with a sly smile said, "I know what to do. I'll give him a vitamin B-12 shot. Those things really hurt. He will think he got some great stuff, and I can keep the important medicines for others."

Quickly Jim filled a syringe with the maximum allowable dose of vitamin B-12. Jim ordered the man to stand and lower his pants so he could give the injection into his hip. Jim swabbed the site with alcohol, pinched up the skin, and jammed in the needle.

"Ouch!" the man exclaimed. He flinched, but bravely stood his ground as Jim pushed in the vitamins as fast as possible and withdrew the needle.

The man fixed his clothing and vigorously rubbed the injection site.

"That *huuurts*!" he proclaimed! "That must be really good medicine!"

Jim just looked at me and smiled as the man walked away, still rubbing his hip.

As midday approached, we had to turn away many who wanted treatment. We had to pack, eat, and then load up for our trip downriver to Suruh Engkadok—and we still needed to make a house call.

While Jim was treating the sick who came to him, a mother presented asking us to go to her house to treat her daughter. The daughter was too ill, too weak, even to walk to the headman's house, and she was too big for mother to carry. Jim agreed to visit the girl after he completed serving the crowd gathered at the headman's house.

When we met the girl I was surprised at how weak and frail she appeared. She was young, just approaching puberty, and tiny. Her flushed cheeks and red eyes indicated a fever. Her frequent coughing indicated serious bronchial infection. She was listless, tired, and weak, but she was not happy to see us. She pulled her sarong up to her chin and backed away from us as Jim knelt beside her to do a better examination. The mother explained the child had been sick for over a week; now she was not eating and only drinking when mother forced her to take a few sips of sweetened tea from a spoon.

Untrained as I was in medical care, I suggested we take the girl to the nearest medical clinic. It was beyond Tamang, but I thought it wise to do so to save the girl's life. Jim just smiled at me and commented it was unnecessary. He would give her an injection of antibiotic now, and another when we returned from our trip downriver.

I was unconvinced. The girl was seriously ill, I asserted, and weakened from her week-long struggle with the sickness. If she did not get help soon, her life would be in jeopardy. Jim assured me that she would be fine. Antibiotics were rarely administered in these remote areas, so their potency was still very high. A single dose would do wonders, and we could check on her again in three days.

I remained unconvinced. This little girl tugged at my heart. I wanted to do all possible to help her. Jim just smiled, and assured me she would be fine. He ignored my protests, gave her an injection of antibiotic, packed up his medical paraphernalia, and led the way back to our lodgings to pack for the trip down river.

Dining with the Dayaks

Dayaks are marvelously hospitable people. Generous to a fault, they always welcome guests with the best they have to offer. Whenever possible while visiting villages, I would take along extra supplies to assist with meals so I would not be too great a burden on my hosts. However, knowing that we had to walk over ten hours through the rainforest to reach the Sekayam River valley I had brought only a small supply of food from Lokok. I was not a US Marine, accustomed to marching all day with eighty pounds of gear on his back. I normally limited my pack to thirty pounds, so I did not have much to offer my hosts on this trip.

In Lokok I had left a good supply of canned sardines, sugar, and coffee as gifts for Suarno and his family, and these gifts were gratefully received. Nonetheless, Dayaks always offered their best to guests, so we were not served sardines while in Lokok. We were served boiled chicken and rice. This was a proper Dayak meal to set before honored guests.

So, on Saturday evening in Lokok, we ate chicken and rice. On Sunday morning, to fortify us for a long day of ministry we were served boiled chicken and rice. At midday, as we visited in a nearby village after services, we were served boiled chicken and rice. Again, that evening back at Suarno's home by the airstrip, Mrs. Suarno served us a fine supper—of boiled chicken and rice. Finally, early Monday morning, before departure for the Sekayam River valley, Mrs. Suarno served us a hearty meal to give us energy for the trek—fried eggs were added to our boiled chicken and rice.

Things were no different in Suruh Tembawang. We were welcomed to the village with a fine meal of boiled chicken and rice. In the morning, before opening the clinic, we breakfasted on boiled chicken and rice.

After breakfast we expressed our appreciation to the headman for his generosity and for the delicious food. Knowing that it was bad manners to ask for something directly, as Dayaks prefer a more indirect style of requests, Jim and I both inquired if they had any bananas, papaya, or other local fruit. We were told nothing was in season.

I inquired about many ubiquitous jungle vegetables. I explained that Jim and I both really liked these jungle vegetables and enjoyed eating them when visiting Dayak villages. We could not get them in the United States so we eagerly anticipated eating them with our Dayak friends.

My hope was that our host would add some readily available vegetables to our diet. Chicken and rice is delicious, but vegetables and fruit provide important nutrition and variety to the diet. We were hopeful that the headman or his wife would understand and add, at least, some cassava leaves to the menu.

Alas, at our last meal before departure, we feasted on boiled chicken and rice. No vegetables. No fruit. Just boiled chicken and rice. As Jim offered the blessing on the meal, I silently asked God for something different for supper in Suruh Engkadok.

River Travel

Our boat was a dugout canoe hull with planks installed as gunwales to add capacity and stability. It was powered by a Yanmar engine that was connected to a propeller shaft. It drew fuel from a sealed tank that required someone to constantly work a hand pump to push air into the tank as the fuel was sucked into the engine. If the operator forgot to work the air pump or rested too long, a suction would form and prevent fuel from being drawn into the engine. One crew member was designated for this task.

Texas

Our engine crew member was a young lad who enjoyed the freedom of life in the jungle. We never learned his name (Dayaks often are hesitant to reveal their names for fear that knowledge can be used to cast a spell against them), so Jim and I just called him Texas because he was wild as a west Texas wind. A true child of the jungle, he went about his duties in preparing for departure with a huge smile, always looking for an excuse to break into loud laughter. He loved to laugh, and we gave him much about which to laugh. Throughout the trip he stayed close to us, eagerly awaiting the next blunder we would make because of our lack of basic rainforest survival skills.

For example, at one point on the trip, the captain pulled up at a small island in the middle of the river. The island was covered with old bamboo and tree branches that had been washed down from the dry rice fields near the river. The captain wanted to pick up a load of firewood. Since all cooking was done on open fires, firewood was always needed. Finding a good supply like this was too great an opportunity to pass up.

As soon as the boat was secured, the captain and crew grabbed their machetes and began chopping the abundant dry wood into the proper size for stowing on the boat. Not to be seen as useless, Jim and I grabbed a machete, too, and went ashore to lend a hand. Texas immediately began to watch us closely, a hopeful smile flashing across his face as he anticipated that we would soon do something hilarious. He did not have to wait long.

After observing what the captain and his mate were doing, we selected a pile of old, dry bamboo. I selected a long shaft and held it out for Jim to cut it down to size. Texas immediately began to giggle. We could see his white teeth flashing bright from a huge smile even though he tried to cover his mouth in an attempt to conceal the fact that he was laughing at us.

Jim looked at me, hoping I could explain what he was doing that was so funny, but all I could do was shrug. I had no idea what Texas found so amusing.

Confused but determined, Jim grabbed the long bamboo shaft with his left hand and raised the machete high over his head with his right hand. Texas's giggles broke out into huge, raucous laughter. With one hand still over his mouth, trying unsuccessfully to conceal his laughter, and the other holding his belly, he was bent nearly double with laughter.

Jim brought the machete down on the bamboo shaft with a powerful stroke. Jim was a big, strong American, and he put his strength into the blow. Instead of biting deeply into the wood, though, the blade bounced up nearly hitting Jim in the face. Surprised at this, Jim looked at the blade and was stunned to see a huge gap in the edge. A three-inch piece of metal had broken off the edge and was wedged tightly into the bamboo. Both Jim and I were shocked! We had no idea that a piece of wood could tear a chunk of metal out of a blade. Our amazement showed clearly on our faces, and that was all Texas could take.

He began to laugh loudly. Tears of laughter began to run down his cheeks. He sat down on a fallen tree and rolled over, holding his sides with both hands in an effort to control his laughter. The captain and his mate both stopped working to see what was happening. Texas tried repeatedly to explain, but every time he raised his hand to demonstrate how Jim had attacked the bamboo shaft, he convulsed anew with laughter and could not speak.

When all three finally stopped laughing, the captain brought us another machete. He showed us how to hold the bamboo shaft upright and use short, quick strokes angled toward the ground to cut the bamboo. He cut into the shaft with a short, quick stroke, rotated the shaft, and struck again, rotated it a third time, and cut into the shaft. The shaft collapsed into neat, even sections. He picked up another bamboo shaft, handed it to Jim, and then handed him the new machete. The captain walked away smiling and shaking his head as he talked with his mate. The mate laughed, replied in their dialect, and both resumed gathering firewood—still giggling.

By the time we had a stack of bamboo ready to be loaded on the boat, Texas had managed to stop laughing. With a huge smile and an occasional burst of laughter, he showed us how to gather the wood, load it up in our arms, and store it in the boat. By the time we pulled away from the island, Texas had finally stopped laughing.

Mate

Our second crew member, I'll called Mate, sat up in the bow with a long pole. His job was to call directions to the captain so he could avoid the rocks, trees, and other debris that had been washed into the river by the heavy rainfall. He always had a long pole in his hand to push the bow away from obstacles in the water, aiding the captain in steering though the rapids and between the trees and other obstacles in the water.

He was a very competent mate. The captain did not need to worry about mate doing his job. Mate could see what needed to be done, do it, and get back to his position in the bow without a word from the captain. An incident that occurred on our return trip to Suruh Tembawang demonstrates this.

Traveling downstream on our boat was easy. The force of the current assisted the single propeller and the Yanmar engine. The return trip, though, had the force of the current working against the engine. The engine did fine in the calm waters, but when we entered the rapids, the engine was barely able to keep us moving forward. Often Mate and Texas would jump over the side to push the boat forward against the current. Captain would have the engine roaring at full speed, but the current, when forced between the rocks would often overpower the engine. If the men had not entered the water, reducing the weight of the boat, and added their strength to the forward motion, the boat might have capsized.

When these incidents occurred, Jim and I remained quietly in the center of the boat. Several times, Caming and Mustafa leaped into the water to assist, as the current was overpowering boat and crew. Their extra strength was welcomed and ensured the boat did not capsize.

On one occasion though, the current was exceptionally strong. Caming and Mustafa leaped into the water to keep us moving forward. Still, even with their added strength, the boat began to slide backward. The current was overwhelming their combined strength. Captain shouted orders, and the men changed positions, shifted some of the baggage to raise the stern—all in an effort to move forward.

Jim and I recognized the danger and prepared to lend a hand. I moved forward into the center of the craft to add stability and held onto the baggage so it would not shift, causing the boat to lean to one side. Jim had been lying in the forward portion of the boat, napping. Hearing the shouts of the crew, and feeling the sideways movement of the boat, he sat up to see what was happening.

"Should I get out and help?" he shouted to Captain, but everyone ignored him. All were totally focused on saving the boat.

Eager to help, Jim moved his feet preparing to leap into the water to add his strength to the fight. His left foot hit the gunwale, breaking it lose from the crossbeam to which it was nailed. The board swung out from the boat and began to catch the water rushing downstream and directing it into the boat. Buckets of water began to flow in, threatening to swamp the boat in seconds.

Seeing the danger, and screaming at Jim to sit down, Mate leaped across the boat, landing unerringly on the rocks. He kicked the board back into place, and slapped the nail back into the crossbeam with his hand. Bracing his feet on the rock and grasping the crossbeam with both hands he gave a mighty shove. Gradually the boat began to move forward. Mate held on, straining with all his might to move the boat. Caming and Mustafa each grabbed a rock on opposite sides of the boat and pulled with all their strength.

Finally, the boat moved forward and out of the narrow passage so that the current lost its force. The propeller again moved the boat forward, and Captain steered it into a quiet spot so we could bail out the water and secure the baggage. No one said anything, but everyone knew Mate saved the boat.

When all was secure, Mate looked at Jim and me like a school principle looking at misbehaving first graders. We both felt ashamed—I because I was not able to help and Jim because in his desire to help he had only made things worse.

"If it happens again," Mate said, "just sit still and let us take care of the boat."

Without another word, he returned to his position in the bow as we resumed our journey. Mate was not one to waste words.

Captain

Captain was a handsome Dayak man. Smooth, even, white teeth flashed brightly from his wide smile. Short, when compared to Jim and me, he was muscular, strong, and energetic. He was never at a loss when traveling the river. The shoals and rapids that filled the riverbed were old friends to him. He knew them well and skillfully steered the boat safely through them. The downed trees that appeared after each rainstorm just added a little excitement to his day, testing his skill and reaction time, keeping him alert as he took us down the river and then back to Suruh Tembawang.

He was a man of surprising strength and agility, with the complete confidence of a young man at the peak of his physical abilities. One of the challenges he faced every night of our trip was how to safely secure his boat engine. It was a Yanmar engine—well built, strong, and heavy. Jim and I, working together, could move it easily. Alone, it was a struggle to lift. Each of us could do it, but it left us panting for breath after only a short walk. That Yanmar was heavy.

One of the biggest problems in a Dayak village is theft. There is a magical power (*ilmu*) at work in most Dayak villages. Things grow legs and walk away. For example, the durable and expensive ironwood planks on major bridges grow legs and walk away. They rarely remain in place for more than a week. Even when nailed down with large, powerful nails, these planks just walk away. In the United States we often joke that if something is not nailed down, it will walk away, but in the Dayak village even things nailed down will walk away. It is powerful magic.

So, Captain knew that he could never leave his fine Yanmar engine in the boat overnight. Every night of our trip, as we off-loaded our gear, I would see Captain disconnect the driveshaft from the propeller so he could take the engine into his sleeping quarters. Leaving it anywhere else would give opportunity to the village magic.

Getting that Yanmar out of the boat was not easy. The banks of the river were steep. When the heavy tropical rains unleashed their fury on the rainforest, the water would fill the riverbed up to the top of the banks. Now, during our trip, it was the drier season; so the top of the riverbank was easily six feet above the surface of the water. Getting up onto the riverbank was a challenge for everyone. At the landings we used, villagers had cut steps into the riverbank to facilitate climbing up. Over time, though, the flooded river's current eroded the steps, leaving only slick indentations in the mud. Using those steps was a challenge for the Dayaks and dangerous for Jim and I. A careless step on the muddy riverbank stairway would put a fellow in the river to the delight of all who witnessed the fall.

Jim and I would always secure our backpacks firmly on our backs, grab a walking stick brought for just this purpose, and slowly, carefully, make our way up the stairway. Each time we reached the top of the bank, or descended to the boat successfully, we paused, took a deep breath and praised God that we made it. Traversing that stairway, at each village, made both of us very nervous.

Captain, though, was not fazed in the least. Every night, at every landing, he was the last one to leave the boat. When all people and gear had left the boat and mounted to the top of the riverbank, Captain would single-handedly hoist that Yanmar engine onto his shoulder. He would then turn to the bank, and in one rapid fluid motion run up the stairs to the top of the riverbank. No hesitation. No quick prayer for help. He just stepped out of the boat on to the first step and ran up the stairway. Every time, when he saw Jim and I watching in amazement, he would just smile and walk away—leaving Jim and I to shake our heads in wonder at the strength, skill, and agility of this Dayak captain. He was an amazing man.

Chapter 11

Suruh Engkadok, Tamang, and the Return to Lokok

Our arrival in Suruh Engkadok village was not a surprise. Somehow, word had reached the village that we were coming. When we pulled in at the landing, late in the afternoon, we were met by a group of laughing, excited children. A few ran on ahead to announce our arrival to the village, and soon a host of village dignitaries led a crowd to greet us.

Our Reception

The dignitaries ushered us to the headman's house while others eagerly carried our baggage to our sleeping quarters. We were served coffee and crackers as we chatted with the various leaders. We presented our papers, so the headman could document our presence to the police and military officials. We explained our reason for visiting them and what we hoped to do while in the village. We were formally received and given permission to conduct meetings and medical clinics. With the formalities completed and plans made for the evening meeting, we headed to our quarters to clean up and prepare for the evening feast.

The feast was laid on in typical Dayak style. Jim and I were the honored guests. Mustafa and Caming were seated beside us. Captain, Mate, and Texas were present but seated among their friends. Jim and I were seated next to the village headman, so Jim was able to engage him in conversation. I focused my attention on watching the activities of the crowd.

Jim and I fully expected another delicious meal of boiled chicken and rice. It was now the fourth day since our arrival at Lokok, and every meal had been the same boiled chicken and rice but no vegetables or fruit. Each meal was chicken and rice. It was delicious food, but after four days, we longed for some fruit and vegetables. We hoped for something other than chicken, too.

We did not get the fruit or vegetables, but we did get a different meat. A villager had made a successful hunt that day. We had wild deer, instead of chicken, with our rice. The meat was salty, flavorful, and a welcome change from chicken. We praised the successful hunter and had to hear his story of the hunt as we ate. Once again, Jim and I marveled at the skill of the Dayaks in wresting a living from the jungle. Their knowledge of the jungle and its creatures was extensive. They knew what the animals ate, where to find the food supply, where the animals gathered, and where to set their traps or wait in ambush. Even more impressive to Jim and me was their ability to make their own muskets, gunpowder, and bullets. These are remarkable people!

Preaching the Gospel

Again, Caming and Mustafa introduced themselves and us to the crowd that gathered for our meeting. We had decided, though, that Jim would lead the singing. He was an energetic man, easily bored, and constantly talking or moving. He led the singing with an enthusiasm most Dayaks were too timid to emulate, but that all loved. Soon, the crowd was laughing at his jokes, his language mistakes, and his explanations of life in the United States. They loved to hear of the mistakes we made while learning to adapt to Dayak life and of how different our lives were back in the United States. Jim did an excellent job of preparing them to hear the gospel.

When I stood up to speak, the entire group was smiling, eager to hear what I would say. As was my habit, I began with creation, Adam and Eve, the Garden of Eden, and the forbidden fruit. I explained the biblical situation, God's daily visit to Adam and Eve in the cool of the evening, and the free interaction between the Creator and Adam and Eve.

I presented the temptation, the sin, the judgment, and the promise. I explained the difference between spiritual death and physical death. I explained the promise of God to send a child, born of Eve but not of Adam, to fix the problem brought on the race by the sin of Adam.

I explained how God taught Adam and Eve a new way of communicating with Him. Since they would no longer be able to meet Him face-to-face, they must now come to Him with the blood of an animal, such as was killed so the skin could be used to cover their nakedness. Without the shedding of blood, they would not be allowed to approach Him, fulfilling the warning that their sin would bring death and demonstrating that without the shedding of blood there was no forgiveness of sin, as stated in Hebrews 9:22, "And according to the law almost all things are purified with blood, and without shedding of blood there is no remission."

As quickly as possible I traced the line of the Seed from Seth to Noah to Abraham to Jesus. I stressed the message of John the Baptist, "Behold the lamb of God who takes away the sin of the world!" (Jn 1:29)

I explained the death and resurrection of Jesus, and his work in opening the way to the Father, the Creator, for all the children of Adam and Eve—Americans and Dayaks. I shared some of the miracles Jesus performed to demonstrate that he had the power to do what he promised and to prove that he was, beyond all doubt, the Promised One. I shared the virgin birth to demonstrate he was the child of Eve, but not of Adam.

I shared the promise of receiving the blessing of the Creator now, in this life, and in the life to come. I invited them to ask Jesus to forgive their sins, transfer them from the Kingdom of Satan to the Kingdom of God, and to deliver them from the power of sin. I offered them peace with God, power over the evil spirits, and God's blessing.

It was a long sermon. I spoke for over an hour. The crowd, though, sat quietly and listened intently. I was the messenger, simply explaining the word of God. The Holy Spirit was present to convict of sin, righteousness, and judgment as Jesus promised.

> Nevertheless I tell you the truth. It is to your advantage that I go away; for if I do not go away, the Helper will not come to you; but if I depart,

I will send Him to you. And when He has come,
He will convict the world of sin, and of righteousness, and of judgment. (Jn 16:7–9)

Caming and Mustafa were present to correct my
language mistakes, compare the scriptural teaching to
the Dayaks' *adat lama* (old ways, traditional culture),
and lead those who believed in the sinner's prayer.

After I sat down, hot tea was served. Jim and I
chatted with the village headman, but I left most of the
conversation to Jim. Jim was a talker, and conversation
was something he loved. I had just spoken for a long
time, so I preferred to sit quietly and listen after I spoke.
By listening, I could learn where my message was misunderstood, discover new words, and better ways of
presenting the message. I could learn more about the
adat lama, enabling me to speak more effectively into
the Dayak worldview with the gospel of Jesus Christ.

I never knew how many professed faith, but Caming
and Mustafa assured me that many believed in Jesus.
It was all for which I hoped. The gospel was preached.
Some believed. It was a good service.

On the morrow, after a breakfast of boiled chicken
and rice (the deer was entirely consumed the night
before), with no vegetables in spite of our repeated
statements that we really, really, longed for some good
cassava leaves, Jim received the sick and treated them
as best he could. There was a large crowd, as medicines
were hard to obtain in Suruh Engkadok though illness
was a daily fact of life.

The needs were far greater than Jim could serve.
Word had spread throughout the region that medical
help was available, so many came from remote villages

for a chance to receive treatment for their illnesses. In those days there were no public health clinics available. The only medical assistance was a doctor in the major town far downriver. Taking a sick person for treatment by the doctor required a full day of travel downriver. Arriving after dark meant the doctor's office would be closed and treatment delayed until the next day. Additional costs were incurred by having to spend the night in town. Thus, folks treated their sick at home, only going to the doctor as a last resort—when all else had failed. So, when they heard Jim was serving the sick, the sick came for service.

Jim did his best. He and I sat on the floor in the headman's house to receive those seeking treatment. Jim would talk with them to discern what was needed and do what he could do. Caming and Mustafa would greet folks as they entered and would help with translation as needed. I would gather up the prescribed medicines, put them in a small plastic bag, and hand it to Jim. Jim would present it to the patient and quickly explain how to administer the drugs.

He had a supply of antibiotics, vitamins, aspirin and other pain relievers, sulfa drugs, eye ointments, and salves for skin lesions. Nonetheless, there were always illnesses for which he had no treatment. It was a great disappointment for folks who traveled long distances to be told there was no useful medicine for them. For these, all we could do was pray.

We did our best to minister to the spiritual needs of the folks who came, but it was not always possible. The crowds grew large and impatient. The children were bored. The sick were in pain, often coughing and feverish. We soon realized that no one was listening to our spiritual teaching. They wanted help for their sick, and then they wanted to go home.

By mid-afternoon, we were tired, hot, and frustrated. The needs were immense, and we could do so very little! Yet, the physical needs were minor compared to the spiritual needs. Very few knew the way of salvation. Most only knew the name of Christ but had no idea of His love for them. Nonetheless, it was time for the midday meal and departure for Tamang.

Tamang

After another meal of boiled chicken and rice, graciously provided by our hosts, we departed for Tamang. The trip was uneventful. The water level was higher as more mountain streams fed into the river further downstream. It was easy traveling.

Again, our arrival was expected. The news had spread, and the village headman was waiting to receive us. We completed the usual formalities, were taken to the place prepared for us, and then invited to dine with the headman. As always, they served us the best they had—boiled chicken and rice.

We asked about the condition of their rice fields, the price of rubber, and what fruits were in season. We wanted to get to know them, but we also wanted to know if there were any fruits or vegetables available to supplement our diet. Regrettably, no fruits were in season, and there were no bananas ready to be harvested.

We asked about cassava leaves and emphasized how much we enjoyed this vegetable. Again, they informed us that they could not serve such meager fare to guests. It was really inappropriate to serve common food to honored guests. In spite of our assurances that we really enjoyed the jungle greens, it was not served during our visit. Jim and I were very disappointed.

Our experience in Tamang was identical with that in Suruh Engkadok and Suruh Tembawang. Jim led the crowd in singing. I preached the gospel, presenting Jesus as the only mediator between God and humanity. All listened intently as I spoke. Caming and Mustafa talked at length with those who were drawn to Jesus. Many were led to offer the sinner's prayer. As we were able, we taught them to read their Bibles, to pray, and to gather every Sunday while one of their own taught the Scriptures. It was the best we could do.

In all three villages, we were asked repeatedly to send someone to stay in the village to teach them the ways of God so they could be good Christians. They wanted to learn. They were willing to erect church buildings and even a parsonage for the minister of the gospel who would come to teach them. We knew that many were more concerned with having medical care available in the village than they were about the gospel. We knew that they only understood the forms of the Christian faith—the singing, the reading of the Bible, the preaching, the prayers, but they did not understand the idea of a personal relationship with their Creator. Nonetheless, they were willing to accept Jesus and to learn to walk in His ways. They just wanted someone to teach them.

The best we could do was to assure them that we would return as God enabled us. We assured them that leaders from Lokok would visit them, based on the promises of Caming and Mustafa. We encouraged them to send key men to Lokok to meet Suarno, to learn from him, and to worship with the mature Christians there.

We knew, though, that it was very unlikely that any would make that long, arduous ten-hour trek to Lokok from Suruh Tembawang.

It was far easier for them to travel downriver to the nearest market town. As we discussed this with the leaders of all three villages, we realized there was a great opportunity for us in the market town, Balai Karangan. Jim and I agreed together that we would work on opening a ministry there so we could develop a consistent ministry to these villages.

In Tamang I preached the gospel to the crowd that gathered that night. I presented the same basic message as I presented in the previous villages. The response was similar. Many were interested. Many had questions that Caming and Mustafa did their best to answer. When necessary, they would ask me for advice before replying to the question.

In the morning Jim served the sick. Many came. All received what Jim was able to give.

After another meal of boiled chicken and rice, we loaded up the boat. Captain and crew took us back to Suruh Engkadok for another night of preaching and a morning of serving the sick—and two more meals of boiled chicken and rice. No fruit. No vegetables. Just a midday meal of chicken and rice, and an evening meal of the same fare.

We purchased some things in Tamang to share with our hosts, but they deemed it inappropriate to serve these things to us. They wanted to give us the best they had, not something anyone could get from the local store. So, it was chicken and rice! I thanked God for their love, kindness and hospitality—while longing for some fruit or vegetables. Some canned sardines and instant noodles would have been a wonderful change, but our gracious hosts wanted to serve us their best.

Suruh Tembawang

Finally, we returned to Suruh Tembawang. We arrived late in the day, just in time for an evening meal of chicken and rice before I again preached the gospel. After the service we announced that we would be leaving early in the morning for our long trek back to Lokok, so there would be no more medical service provided. We thanked the village leaders and the entire assembly for their kindness and hospitality and dismissed the crowd.

After the crowd dispersed, we gave gifts to Captain, Mate, and Texas. They had worked hard on this trip, all in an effort to help us preach the gospel. They did not ask for money for fuel or wages for their time, but we knew it had cost them time and money to ferry us downriver and back. We offered them suitable gifts and thanked them profusely for their assistance.

After we had prayed with them, Captain and Texas left for their own homes. Mate lingered to talk further with us.

"Everyone in the village is excited about you coming to visit us," Mate began. "We all appreciate the medicines, the teaching, and the good times we had visiting with you. Your stories are funny, and they make people laugh. We want to show you our appreciation for all you have done."

"You have been wonderful to us!" Jim replied. "You have fed us, and given safe places to sleep, and helped us with our travel. You do not need to do anything more for us!"

"Well," Mate replied, "there is one more thing we would like to do. All the girls think you are very handsome and want to be with you tonight. If you want, I will send some to you."

Confused, Jim and I exchanged glances. In English I asked Jim, "Did he say what I think he said"

"Did he just offer us a couple girls for the night?" he replied.

"Yes, I think he did. Did I misunderstand?" I asked.

"Well, that is what I heard, too. I think he means it!" Jim said. "Have you ever had this happen before?"

"I read about it in my research. Dayaks often offer a girl to a respected guest, but no one has ever actually offered me a girl before now." I stated. "I did not think it was still done."

"We cannot accept!" Jim said emphatically.

"Of course not!" I replied. "I just wanted to be sure I understood him correctly before I replied. If I misunderstood his offer I might say the wrong thing and make a big mess of this."

Turning to Mate, and speaking in Indonesian, I explained that while I appreciated the offer, and that the girls of the village were indeed beautiful and desirable, it would not be appropriate for us to accept. I explained that we were both married and that we had promised to be faithful to our wives. I further explained that this was the requirement of God, as revealed in the Bible, and that we simply could not accept his offer.

Mate urged us to accept the offer, explaining that the girls would be very disappointed and embarrassed if we declined. The village would think that they were not pretty enough, or too dark-complected for us. He really thought it would be best if we each accepted a girl for the night.

I assured him the girls were beautiful, and that our decision to decline the offer in no way implied that we did not admire them. I stated again that we were married and that our God and our wives expected us to be faithful to our wives.

I do not think Mate ever really understood or agreed with our decision, but eventually he accepted it and left for his home.

Our early departure was delayed. Our gear was packed up, and our packs were ready. We were eager to start on our way, but the headman insisted we could not leave without a good breakfast. The chicken was already in the pot, and the rice was cooking. We were served coffee and told, *Sabarlah*! (Be patient!). Breakfast would soon be served.

While waiting, the father of the little girl who had been very sick the day we departed for Suruh Engkadok came to us. He said the girl was better, but he wanted Jim to give her another injection of medicine before we left to be sure the illness would not return. Jim and I both remembered how listless and weak the child had been. Since we had time, Jim prepared another injection of the antibiotic, and we followed the father to his house.

As we approached the house we saw the girl playing on the veranda. She looked up as we approached, and her father spoke to her in their local language. The girl immediately leaped off the veranda, jumped over the fence around the house, and disappeared into the jungle! I was amazed that one shot of antibiotic was so powerful! One dose, and in four days that girl was strong enough to flee another injection by running away into the jungle!

"Well," Jim said, "She is more afraid of the injection than she is of being sick. I don't think she needs any more medicine." We returned to the headman's house for breakfast, and then set out for Lokok.

The Return to Lokok

Our trek back to Lokok was uneventful. We arrived ten hours after departure, well after sunset. Since we were back in the Lokok area, Caming and Mustafa had no difficulty finding their way through the rainforest in the dark. They knew the trails well. They escorted us to the airstrip, paused only long enough to ensure we could see Suarno's house at the other end of the strip, and then disappeared into the darkness, eager to reach their own homes.

Our Welcome

Suarno was anxious about us. He had expected us to arrive before nightfall and was concerned that something had gone wrong. There were many things that could have delayed us—a special event or illness in Suruh Tembawang, an injury on the trail, or taking the wrong trail. Many things could go wrong in the jungle. So it was a great relief to him when we hello-ed the house to announce our arrival. His exuberant welcome lifted our spirits, and the hot *kopi susu* he had waiting for us renewed our energy.

After coffee and a brief rest, Jim and I headed down the mountainside for a *mandi* (Caming told us on the morrow that he heard us screaming at the cold water!), and by the time we returned, Mrs. Suarno had supper laid out for us. Her delight in serving us was evident, as she had prepared some special treats for us! Chicken and rice! Jim and I complimented her cooking and asked if she had any cassava leaves in the kitchen. Surprised at our request, but gracious as always, she served the vegetables. She shook her head in confusion at our excitement over this jungle staple.

Sunday Worship

The church was filled to overflowing for Sunday worship service. Everyone wanted to hear our report of events in the Sekayam River valley. Caming and Mustafa shared their insights about the trip. They emphasized that many came to faith in Jesus. Caming even gave a summary of the message I preached in each village, and shared how it strengthened his own faith.

Mustafa kept the crowd laughing with his accounts of Jim and me opening the can of cheese by beating it on the rock. The laughter was even more raucous as he told how Jim nearly sank the boat by kicking the gunwale into the current.

Jim preached a gospel message. He shared that while most of his work on the trip was healing the physical bodies of our friends living on the banks of the Sekayam River, their greatest need was for healing of their spiritual disease of sin. He explained how Jesus was the healing balm of Gilead that could restore their personal relationship with their Creator.

After the service ended, and the worshippers had departed for their homes, Mrs. Suarno served us another fine meal. Chicken and rice! Again, she had to be persuaded to include the cassava leaves on the menu. She did not feel comfortable serving her guests such simple food. She wanted to give us something better than their daily fare. We explained that we needed the nutrition of the dark green vegetable and that it was a delicious addition to the menu. She could understand why we eagerly ate the bananas someone had brought to share with their pastor and us, but she just could not understand why we wanted the cassava leaves.

After dinner, Jim and I walked to a nearby village to join in the volleyball games with the young folks. Neither of us was very good. The kids welcomed us, though, knowing that we would be a source of great laughter as we tried to play the game. It was a good time of relaxed interaction with the young folks, and it helped us improve our language and understanding of Dayak culture.

We stayed for supper in the village, dining with the church elders who normally led the Sunday evening Bible study. After the food and dishes were cleared, folks began to wander in for the meeting. Jim led the singing, and I spoke from the Scriptures. In these meetings, knowing that most, if not all, present were believers in Jesus, I emphasized basic Bible doctrines, the nature of God (as opposed to the nature of Jubata, the rice god), the importance of Christian living (especially integrity and chastity), and faith in God to provide for daily needs. I also emphasized the need for disciples of Jesus to share their faith and train others to do the same. It was just basic Christian teaching, but it was what they needed.

After the message, the ladies served everyone coffee or tea, sticky rice, fried cassava with molasses, and local fruit. We talked and sang more songs, exchanged stories—just enjoying the friendship of these wonderful people. Finally, long after moonrise, we headed back to Suarno's house. Our work, for this trip, was done. All that remained was the flight back to Pontianak in the morning.

Home!

We had requested that our return flight be scheduled for early in the morning. We knew that after eight days in the village, we would be eager to go home. However, the flight schedule for this week had not been finalized when we left Pontianak, so we really did not know when the flight would arrive. We just knew we had to be ready when it came.

MAF could not fly before the sun had burned off the morning ground fog, so the first flight rarely left Supadio, the airport serving Pontianak, before nine o'clock in the morning. Flight time from Supadio to Lokok was about forty-five minutes, so Jim and I knew the plane would not reach Lokok before ten o'clock. We also knew that many things could delay the flight and that bad weather could cause the flight to be canceled altogether. All we could do was wait for the plane to arrive.

Nonetheless, we were up, packed, and ready to go by eight o'clock in the morning. We were ready to go home! Of course, we had our early morning *mandi* and our morning *kopi susu* with Suarno. We read the Scriptures and prayed with him before enjoying our delicious breakfast—chicken and rice with fried eggs and sardines in tomato sauce. She even served the cassava leaves without us having to ask for it. To top it all off, she had prepared doughnuts! Really! Doughnuts!! She was a wonderfully kind and gracious hostess.

By nine o'clock all the details were completed. Bags were packed and stacked by the shed at the top end of the airstrip. Farewells had been said, and appreciation expressed for all who had assisted us. Gifts of appreciation had been given and received. It was time to go. For a long time, we sat on the veranda, listening for the sound of the approaching plane. We scanned the sky to the west, looking for a small dot that would indicate the plane was coming. Nervously, we scanned the horizon in all directions, fearing we would see thunderclouds building up that would prevent the plane from flying in to Lokok. The sun continued to shine, and the bright blue sky remained cloudless, but the plane did not come.

By noon the villagers who had come to see us off and wish us safe journey, and who hoped to see the plane, had tired of waiting. The work in the fields needed to be done, so they departed to their own places. Jim and I sat on the veranda and impatiently searched the sky for the plane. Eventually, I rested my head on my backpack and fell asleep.

It was after one o'clock in the afternoon when the plane finally arrived. We quickly loaded our gear and gave our final farewells. The weather was threatening to cut us off from Pontianak, so the pilot wanted to depart as quickly as possible. We raced the storm clouds to Supadio and were safely in the hanger when the rain hit. In Indiana they are called "severe thunderstorms" and cause much concern. The weather reports would warn everyone to take cover until the severe weather passed. At Supadio, though, it was just the daily afternoon rain; so Jim and I took a taxi back to my home in Pontianak.

Carolyn was waiting for us. She had been in contact with MAF and knew we had arrived at Supadio. She knew it would take about an hour for us to reach our home from Supadio, so she had arranged a great "welcome home" meal for us. She led us into the dining room where the meal was laid out for us on the table—chicken and rice!

Jim and I did not know what to say. We just stood there looking at this wonderful meal that Carolyn had worked so hard to prepare for us. Any other day we would have been delighted to eat this meal. But not today. Not today!

Finally, I spoke.

"Carolyn, we have eaten chicken and rice twice a day for the last ten days. We can't do it again! Have the helper put it in the refrigerator. We're going to a restaurant."

God gave me a wife perfectly suited for the work to which He called us. She understood immediately and completely. Laughing out loud, she called the helpers and told them what to do. In a short time, Carolyn, Jim, and I were feasting on pork cooked in soy sauce, sweet-and-sour pork, and stir-fried vegetables—two full plates of stir-fried vegetables! It was *great* to be home!

Our trip had been completed without major difficulty. The team suffered no injuries or sickness, and many had come to faith. Many more had heard the gospel but would need further teaching and careful thought before they would be ready to break with their old ways. We had met the key leaders in these river villages and established working relationships with them. We had standing invitations to return to preach, teach, and serve the sick. It was a very successful trip in every way.

Chapter 12

Epilogue

Jim and I were convinced that God had granted us a great opportunity to reach the unreached people of West Kalimantan. We knew it would be difficult to continue the work we had started, but we were absolutely convinced that it could be done. We were convinced that by God's grace we could train the leaders in Lokok to make monthly visits to the Sekayam River valley. These leaders, like Caming and Mustafa, could train the spiritual leaders in the villages we visited to make disciples who made more disciples. We could train them to lead new churches in their own villages and to reach out to other villages in the valley. After our return to Pontianak, we began to put these plans into action. There were greater challenges than we anticipated, though.

Jim's Second Trip to the Sekayam River Valley

Two months after our ministry in the Sekayam River valley, I returned to the United States for a year of Home Ministry Assignment (HMA). This was an essential part of missionary service. We had to report to our financial donors and to our prayer supporters about what had been accomplished. We also had to raise additional funds for our financial needs. As members of a faith mission (a mission organization that is not supported by a specific denomination), we were responsible to raise all the funds we used. If we did not raise these funds, our ministry would end. So, HMA was essential, and I had to return to the United States.

We agreed that while I was in the United States, Jim would begin the training program in the Sekayam valley. When I returned, it would be time for Jim to return to Australia for his HMA, and I would take up the task of training disciples to make disciples in the Sekayam valley. Jim's second visit to the Sekayam valley did not go well, however.

The trek over the mountains to Suruh Tembawang went smoothly. The Lokok church appointed men to make the trip with Jim. These leaders were eager to preach the gospel and to learn from Jim how to lead the church. Captain and Mate were again available and willing to make the trip down river to Tamang, so the gospel could be preached.

The boat trip down river went smoothly, also. The river was high from recent rains and the current was strong. The high water level made it easier to pass the rapids and to avoid the fallen trees and other debris in the riverbed.

The ministry in Suruh Tembawang and Suruh Engkadok was well received. The villagers eagerly welcomed Jim, and the meetings were well attended. Jim provided his usual medical care, and many came for treatment. More importantly, in these villages Jim held the first leadership training programs. Jim began teaching the men and women who were serious about their faith and willing to study the Scriptures on a regular basis. These would become the leaders of the churches in each village.

Jim explained our plans for monthly visits by leaders from Lokok to teach these leaders what they were learning back in Lokok. Jim would visit Lokok once a month and train the Lokok leaders to teach specific lessons. Trained leaders would then travel to the Sekayam valley to teach the lessons to their leaders. Once every three months, Jim would make the trek to Sekayam to teach and encourage the leader, and also to offer medical assistance.

It was a good plan. Jim would get things started. I would continue it when I returned from the United States. When Jim returned from his HMA, we would share the load. Each of us would make two visits to Sekayam every year. All were confident this would lead to rapid growth of the Kingdom of God in the Sekayam River Valley.

The believers in Tamang were excited about this plan as well, and were eager to participate—until a local police official intervened.

The Police Order

News of our visit to these three villages had traveled down river to Balai Karangan, the major market town and seat of government in the valley. From Balai Karangan one could travel by road to Kembayan and Sosok. Sosok was on the main highway in West Kalimantan—and just a few miles from my home in Jelimpo.

The Snowy Mountain Engineering Company, based in Australia, had received a contract funded by the United Nations to build a paved road from Pontianak, the provincial capital, to Sintang. This great east-west highway would improve the economy of the province and living standards of the people by facilitating the sale of vast natural resources from the jungle, like rubber and lumber, to eager businesses on the coast. It would also facilitate the shipment of consumer goods into the growing cities in the interior.

Balai Karangan was the link to the outside world for the Sekayam valley people. The government had opened administrative, police, and military offices here. It was an important and growing town. People traveled from far upriver to sell their goods and purchase what they could not build or grow for themselves in their jungle villages.

The chief of police in Balai Karangan was responsible for the security of the region. It was a serious responsibility. When news reached him of two foreigners preaching and selling medicines in the villages upriver, he was concerned. He decided to travel upriver to investigate these reports, to meet the village leaders, and to assess the situation there. So it was that Jim met the chief of police in Tamang.

The meeting did not go well for Jim. He had reported to the headman of Tamang when he arrived, presenting the Indonesian documents he normally carried when traveling. However, these documents were insufficient for the chief of police. He wanted to see Jim's passport, his visa to enter Indonesia, and his residence card (KIMS). He also wanted a travel letter from the police in the area where Jim resided and a document from the provincial Department of Religion, verifying Jim's identity and permission to serve the people of the Sekayam valley.

The passport and KIMS were safely stored in our offices in Pontianak. The risk of losing them was too great for them to be carried about on our person. Since Jim had visited these villages previously, he had not obtained a travel letter from his own village headman or local police. Nor had he made the long trip to Pontianak to request a travel letter from the Department of Religion. Jim explained his purpose for visiting the region and assured the officer that he would comply with his requirements on all future visits. Jim asked the officer to overlook his lack of proper papers on this trip and assured him proper papers would be presented on subsequent visits to this area.

The officer rebuked Jim strongly, informing Jim that he was subject to arrest for traveling without proper documents. The officer was willing to accept Jim's explanations, and he believed it unnecessary to arrest Jim. However, he informed Jim, in the strongest possible terms, that on all future visits to these villages Jim must appear at the police office in Balai Karangan before he traveled to the villages. If Jim walked into the valley from Lokok, Jim was not allowed to spend even one night in a village on the river until he had traveled to Balai Karangan and reported to the chief of police. He further insisted that Jim and his companions leave immediately in the morning to return to Lokok. Finally, he ordered that no meeting was to be held in Tamang that night, and Jim was not to dispense any medicines. Failure to comply would result in the arrest of Jim and his companions—those from Lokok as well as those from Suruh Tembawang.

Jim had no choice but to comply with these orders from the chief of police. In the morning, Jim and his colleagues expressed their regret to the people of Tamang and departed for Suruh Engkadok.

The Capsized Boat

The water level in the river was high due to recent rains, so the current remained very strong. Travel upstream was slow and difficult. This forced them to spend the night in Suruh Engkadok. The villagers expected a meeting to be held, and they wanted more medicines in the morning. But Jim explained the orders he had received from the chief of police and asked the village headman to forgive him for not serving the village as he had done in the past. The headman understood the problem and agreed with Jim's decision not to lead a worship service or conduct a medical clinic. He himself had received a letter from the chief of police, instructing him not to allow us to do anything in the village under pain of his own arrest and removal from office as the village headman.

Again, frustrated but powerless, Jim and team boarded the boat and set out for Suruh Tembawang. The current remained strong. The powerful Yanmar motor struggled to make headway in the rapids. The crew was frequently forced to go over the side into the water to add their own strength to that of the engine before the boat could pass the rapids.

While crossing one these rapids, the boat capsized. Men and material all went into the water. Many of the trade goods were washed away, heading down river at great speed, destined to be picked up by a lucky villager downstream. The sugar, salt, and coffee were spoiled—as was the tea and rice. The captain's greatest loss, though, was his homemade flintlock musket. Captain and crew searched the riverbed for the musket, but it was not found.

More than anything else, Captain regretted the loss of that musket. It was illegal to have a musket, but the Dayaks still hunted in those mountainous areas. Wild bore still roamed the jungles, and fresh meat was a welcome addition to the menu. Captain knew he could make another one, but the time and cost of materials would make it an expensive process.

The Alternative Route

After my return from HMA and before Jim left for his own HMA, we met to determine a course of action. Jim had been training the Lokok leaders, but the trips to the Sekayam valley by the Lokok leaders had not been continued. Without our participation, the Lokok folks were reluctant to make the long trip to the Sekayam valley. An alternative plan was needed.

The requirement for us to report to the chief of police in Balai Karangan was a problem, but we realized there was a viable solution. I could reach Balai Karangan by road from my home in Jelimpo in three hours. It would be much cheaper and faster to travel by road to Balai Karangan. We could report ministry plans to the chief of police, meet Captain and Mate at scheduled times, travel upriver for ministry, then return via Balai Karangan. This alternative route had many advantages, so we agreed that I would act to redeem this opportunity while Jim was on HMA.

Balai Karangan

Recognizing that Jim and I had not appropriately handled the relationships with local officials in Balai Karangan before our first visits to the Sekayam River Valley, I was determined to do things properly as we pursued this alternative route to the valley. Our goals were to establish the Body of Christ in the valley; to train local church leaders to lead the church and evangelize the villages not on the river itself; and to serve the people with medical and educational assistance. These were worthy goals, and we were confident the government officials in Balai Karangan would support our plans, or, at least, not hinder them.

I arranged meetings with our mission team and national church leaders to share our vision. After hearing the reports of what had been done and our plans for moving forward, there was unanimous agreement that the plans should be implemented as soon as possible. To facilitate this, mission and church leaders would join me in a trip to Balai Karangan to meet with the chief of police, the military leaders, and other important leaders. All were convinced that personal meetings would establish relationships essential to fulfillment of our goals.

On the agreed date, the team gathered at my home in Jelimpo. We spent the evening in prayer, asking God to grant us safe travel and favor in the eyes of the government officials in Balai Karangan. Our six-member team included the head of our national denomination and his secretary, our national church district leader for the Jelimpo area, our mission field director, the director of our inter-mission business office (our liaison with the government offices in Pontianak), and me. Jim was still out of Indonesia on HMA.

We reached Balai Karangan as the offices were opening, in hopes that we could arrange meetings with all the officials in one day. The Indonesian team and our mission field director entered the offices to arrange the meetings and present our plans. Our office manager, Eric, and I remained nearby, ready to assist if requested.

It was a long day. The team met with many officials from the various government agencies involved. Papers were presented, relationships discovered, and new ones formed. It was business done the Indonesian way. Regrettably, it failed.

Our team was informed that we were not allowed to visit the Sekayam River valley for any reason. If we did so, we would be arrested and subject to legal action. Why?

There were several official reasons given. First, our initial entry into the area had been done improperly. Jim and I should have contacted the Balai Karangan officials before making that first visit to the area. Clearly, the local leadership was offended by our breach of protocol.

Second, the local officials expressed concern for our safety. The Dayaks were headhunters and cannibals, they said. The police would not be able to assure our safety if we visited the remote upriver villages. If something bad happened, they would be held accountable by their superiors for failing to protect us. So, they did not want us to visit the region without a police escort.

Third, the Sekayam River is very close to the border with Malaysia. Under the Sukarno administration, a *konfrontasi* (confrontation) had escalated to an "undeclared war" between Malaysia and Indonesia.[9] The military officials feared the presence of foreigners in the region would prove unsettling to the local population on both sides of the border. Any violence in the region would reflect poorly on them and could have international consequences. The military officials did not want us visiting the area without military or police escort.

None of these reasons made any sense to me. Admittedly, Jim and I had entered the region without first contacting the local officials in Balai Karangan. Technically, we did not have to do so. Our work was authorized and approved by the governor's office, the provincial military and police leadership, and the provincial Department of Religion. This approval and authorization was renewed annually in Pontianak, the provincial capital. We had done nothing illegal. The failure was one of protocol only, and we were now trying to rectify the error by consulting with the local officials.

The Dayaks did have a history of headhunting and cannibalism. On occasion, violence would break out among them. Yet, our mission team had lived and worked among the Dayaks since 1948 without incident. We were viewed as friendly advocates of the Dayak people. We were known for helping the Dayaks with medical care, education, community development, and opening avenues for participation in the larger world. We had nothing to fear from the Dayaks. Besides, they are just good people. Treat them with respect, and they will respond in the same way.

The *konfrontasi* had ended fourteen years before. The Suharto administration had ended the conflict and developed amicable governmental and economic relationships with Malaysia. There was no tension in the region. Our team was convinced there was another reason for the ban. We just did not know what it was.

Ministry Halted

Months later, Captain made an overland trip to Serimbu. While there he met one of our Canadian colleagues who lived in the area. Initially, Captain thought my Canadian colleague was me. After sorting out the identities, they began to discuss ministry in the Sekayam valley.

My colleague inquired if any Christian ministry was being done in the region. Captain explained that leaders from another denomination had visited Suruh Tembawang, Suruh Engkadok, and Tamang with a contingent of policemen. The religious and police leaders explained that these villages were now being served by this different denomination. When they left, they posted signs stating that the village was being served by this denomination, and all other denominations were forbidden to minister there. In the six months since the signs were posted, no one had returned to lead services. No ministry of any kind had been conducted.

Two years later, I was privileged to return to Lokok for ministry. During my time there, I inquired about what was happening in the Sekayam River villages. The news was not good. Since the signs were posted, no one had returned to preach the gospel or train disciples in the villages. No one had been baptized. No one had served the Lord's Supper. No marriages had been blessed. The believers no longer met regularly, and many had returned to their old ways. The other denomination, with police help, banned us from making disciples in the region, but failed to do any ministry there.

I was angry. Satan had used this other denomination to block the progress of the gospel! Of course, I said nothing to anyone except to Jesus. I unleashed my anger in prayer, asking the Lord to change the situation. I prayed for wisdom and courage to do what could be done, so these villages would not again fall under the control of the enemy of our souls and enter a new spiritual Dark Age. Finally, I had an idea.

A Second Attempt

A new missionary family had moved to Jelimpo. It was important that I introduce the new ordained minister to the believers in the area and show him around. So, he and I took a motorcycle ride to Balai Karangan. I wanted to see how the town had changed. Perhaps new officials were in place, so we could renew our work in the area.

My friend and I arrived about noon. I led the way up the main street, just looking at the buildings, stores, and offices. When we came to the river, I turned back into the market place and looked for a coffee shop.

As we were driving slowly up the street, I heard a commanding voice calling something. Surprised, I stopped and looked back to see who was calling. A police officer was approaching, clearly wanting to speak with us. We shut down our engines and waited for him to speak.

"Where are you from?" he asked.

"From Jelimpo, Pak. A village near Sosok." I replied.

"When did you arrive here?"

"Just now."

"Did you report to the police?" he asked.

"Not yet," I replied. "We wanted to get something to drink first."

"Report in first," he said. "Afterwards you can drink."

"Fine, sir. Where is the police office?" I replied.

"Follow me." he instructed.

In the office we were seated before the officer's desk and required to show our Indonesian Driver's License as identification. The details were recorded, along with our place of residence, purpose of our travel, and estimated time we would be in town. Learning that we were working with a specific denomination in the neighboring district, the officer informed us that the other denomination was serving this area. Our denomination was not needed. We should stay out of the area.

After being released by the officer, we had sweetened iced tea at a coffee shop in the market place. Angry and disappointed, we considered our options. We concluded there really was nothing to be done at this time. Perhaps we could approach the head of the Department of Religion in Pontianak for assistance. However, I knew that the department head was friendly with the denomination controlling the Sekayam valley and with the chief of police in Balai Karangan. It was doubtful we would receive any assistance from the gentleman. We concluded we could only leave it in God's hands. Only God could break down the wall Satan had constructed to prevent the gospel being preached and the Kingdom of God being enlarged in the Sekayam River valley.

When we finally left Indonesia in 1990, no one, to the best of our knowledge, had renewed ministry in the Sekayam River valley. Not one visit had been made to Suruh Tembawang, Suruh Engkadok, or Tamang. It was not the first time, nor the last, when other denominations used political connections to banish us from ministries we had initiated. In every instance, the other organization did not continue the ministry as promised. The villages were left without gospel witness.

Lesson Learned

What lesson did I learn from this? If I promise to do something—visit a village, preach somewhere, conduct a training seminar—I must keep my promise. The other denomination promised to evangelize the Sekayam River valley and to make disciples there, but they did not do it. Only God knows how many passed into a Christless eternity because of such evil actions and broken promises.

PART 4

Conclusion

Chapter 13

LESSONS LEARNED

M y purpose in writing this text was to answer the question: "Why are you Americans able to send missionaries around the world but we Batak Christians cannot do so?" Drawing from various lessons I learned along the way, I have demonstrated from personal experience that the foundation of discipleship, of missionary service, is the principle of the cross. Missionary service is simply discipleship lived out by using the spiritual gifts given to the believer by the Holy Spirit. It is not a function of a specific culture or ethnic group.

The principle of the cross involves three principles of Christian life and ministry that should be part of the life of every believer in Jesus Christ. These principles are:

1. The basis of discipleship is the call of God. This call must be clear and compelling. No one becomes a disciple of Jesus or stays on the mission field without a personal call and a deep commitment to God's work. Without it, people

abandon their faith in Jesus or quit the mission field and go home.

2. The power of discipleship is prayer. Prayer is essential to successful discipleship, and especially to the life and ministry devoted to missionary service. While there are many ways to pray, the critical issue is that one prays. Without a strong prayer life, again, people quit and go home.

3. The methods of discipleship are varied. They must be developed after acquiring a basic understanding of the language and culture of those to whom the disciple is sent to preach the gospel. While it is not easy to acquire a new culture or to learn a new language, it is essential to the evangelization of an unreached people group.

I have told the story of how I served in West Kalimantan. I remain convinced that stories are a better means of communication than propositional teaching, although there is a need for the latter at specific times and places. The stories are easier to remember. They demonstrate the principles in clear, easily understood terms. Every true disciple understands the importance of knowing that God has called him to service. Every true disciple understands the importance of prayer. Every true disciple wants to know how to share his faith with people who do not believe that Jesus is God in the flesh.

These stories are simply presentations of lessons I have learned along the way. I pray that these stories will cause many to remember the principles and apply them in their lives and ministries.

The principle of the cross does not merely mean that we suffer for Jesus by being jailed, tortured, or martyred for His name. The principle of the cross does not just mean that we die for Jesus. It also means that we live for Jesus! It means that our personal goals, aims, plans, desires, and choices are abandoned—nailed to the cross—and replaced with an entirely new set of goals, aims, plans, desires, and choices that come from Christ Himself. These are rooted in His call on our lives and our response of commitment to Him. This is what Christ calls every person who claims to follow Him to do. This is discipleship.

Wayne and Carolyn 2014

We cannot serve two masters. We either pursue our own hopes, dreams, goals, ambitions, and desires, or we pursue the hopes, dreams, goals, ambitions, and desires Christ gives us. This is a fundamental lesson I have learned along the way.

WORKS CITED

Beyer, Cassie. "Slash and Burn Agriculture: Definition and Method." *Study.com* 2017, no. March 15 (2017). http://study.com/academy/lesson/slash-and-burn-in-agriculture-definition-and-method.html.

Emrath, Paul. "How Long Buyers Remain in Their Homes." (2009). http://www.nahbclassic.org/generic.aspx?genericContentID=110770&channelID=311.

Greene, Richard W. "Keystone Project Training Manual." Fort Wayne: World Partners, 2008. Unpublished.

Hindley, Donald. "Indonesia's Confrontation with Malaysia: A Search for Motives." *Asian Survey* 4, no. 6 (1964): 904-13.

Konick, Rodolphe De, Stephane Bernard, and Jean-Francois Bissonnette. *Borneo Transformed: Agricultural Expansion on the Southeast Asian Frontier*. Singapore: NUS, 2011.

Leifer, Michael. "Indonesia and Malaysia: The Changing Face of Confrontation." *The World Today* 22, no. 9 (September 1966): 395-405.

Meister, Jeanne. "Job Hopping Is the 'New Normal' for Millennials: Three Ways to Prevent a Human Resource Nightmare." Forbes.com, http://www.forbes.com/sites/jeannemeister/2012/08/14/job-hopping-is-the-new-normal-for-millennials-three-ways-to-prevent-a-human-resource-nightmare/.

Omar, Marsita. "Indonesia-Malaysia Confrontation." *Singapore Infopedia* (2010). http://eresources.nlb.gov.sg/infopedia/articles/SIP_1072_2010-03-25.html.

Your Dictionary. LoveToKnow, Corp, 2017.

ABOUT THE AUTHOR

B orn on January 19, 1951 in the United States, Wayne W. Allen attended Fort Wayne Bible College to prepare for missionary service, receiving a BA in 1975. He earned an MA from Grace Theological Seminary in 1982, an MA from Fuller Theological Seminary in 1993, and a Doctor of Philosophy (Missiology) degree from Concordia Theological Seminary in 1998.

Wayne W. Allen

Wayne served from 1978 to 1990 as a missionary in West Kalimantan, Indonesia. He worked in village evangelism, trained lay people to serve as pastors in remote villages, and pastored a village church. In 1988 he directed the establishment of a baccalaureate program at Berea Bible Institute, Ansang, Darit. He oversaw development of the curriculum, staff, publicity, and student recruitment. He also served as an instructor.

After serving as lecturer in and chairman of the Department of Missions at Summit Christian College in Fort Wayne, Indiana during 1991-1992, Wayne completed his Ph.D. in Missiology at Concordia Theological Seminary, Fort Wayne, in 1996.

From 1996–2002, Wayne served as the David Ho Professor of World Missions at the Caribbean Graduate School of Theology in Kingston, Jamaica. His primary focus was to train Caribbean people for cross-cultural missionary service.

Beginning in 2003, Wayne worked tirelessly in many Asian countries to launch disciple-making movements. In 2013, Wayne was able to transfer the leadership in these areas to four nationals, two in north India, one in Myanmar, and one in Nepal.

END NOTES

1   Jeanne Meister, "The Future of Work: Job Hopping Is the 'New Normal' for Millennials," (August 14, 2012): accessed January 25, 2017. <http://www. forbes.com/sites/jeannemeister/2012/08/14/the-future-of-work-job-hopping-is-the-new-normal-for-millennials/#6ebc338f322d>.

2   Paul Emrath, "How Long Buyers Remain in Their Homes," National Association of Home Builders (February 11, 2009): accessed January 25, 2017. <http://www.nahbclassic.org/generic.aspx?genericContentID=110770&channelID=311>.

3   Barboncito. (n.d.). accessed March 15, 2017. http://biography.yourdictionary.com/barboncito

4   Our national church was the GPPIK, commonly shortened to PPIK. The full Indonesian name is Gereja Persekutuan Pemberitaan Injil Kristus which RBMU translated as "The Fellowship of Preaching the Gospel of Christ Church."

5   Richard W. Greene, "Keystone Project Training Manual." (Fort Wayne: World Partners, 2008. Unpublished), 74.

6   Green, 74.

7   Rodolphe De Koninck, Stéphane Bernard, and Jean-François Bissonnette, (Singapore: NUS, 2011). 13.

8   *Cassie Beyer*, Slash and burn in Agriculture: Definition and Method. Study.com: accessed March 15, 2017. <http://study.com/academy/lesson/slash-and-burn-in-agriculture-definition-and-method.html>. See also Slash-and-burn agriculture. EcoLogic Development Fund: accessed March 15, 2017. <http://www.ecologic.org/actions-issues/challenges/slash-burn-agriculture>.

9   Indonesia-Malaysia Confrontation. National Library Board (Singapore 2010). accessed March 16, 2017. <http://eresources.nlb.gov.sg/infopedia/articles/SIP_1072_2010-03-25.html>. For further details see Michael Leifer, "Indonesia and Malaysia: The Changing Face of Confrontation," Vol. 22, No. 9 (Sep., 1966), pp. 395-405, and Donald Hindley, "Indonesia's Confrontation with Malaysia: A Search for Motives," Vol. 4, No. 6 (Jun., 1964), pp. 904-913, doi: 10.2307/3023528.